An Invitation
to Self-Care

"No one gets through this life without a few twists and turns, disappointments and surprises. This book gives you the tools to become the architect of your own support system so that you can survive any crisis and learn to thrive again."

—Lee Woodruff, best-selling author of *Perfectly Imperfect*

"As a nutrition and fitness expert, I have seen firsthand how taking care of your health and body can radically change your life for the better. Tracey's new book guides readers to create a powerful self-care program that is uniquely theirs. Whether your goals are physical, emotional, spiritual or mental, you can't miss with this book. You will discover your strengths and areas for growth. By taking excellent care of yourself, you will have the stamina, courage, and energy to live the life you've always dreamed of."

—JJ Virgin, best-selling author of *Sugar Impact Diet* and *The Virgin Diet*

"French women learn from a young age to practice the art of self-care. It's the secret to their famous mystery and confidence. So how can we, as Americans, borrow a little of that savoir-faire and take better care of ourselves? Easy. Read Tracey Cleantis's wonderful book An Invitation to Self-Care. It will change your life!"

—Jamie Cat Callan, author of
French Women Don't Sleep Alone, Ooh La La! and *Bonjour, Happiness!*

An Invitation to Self-Care

Why Learning to Nurture Yourself
Is the Key to the Life You've Always Wanted

7 Principles for Abundant Living

TRACEY CLEANTIS

Hazelden
Publishing

Hazelden Betty Ford Foundation
Center City, Minnesota 55012
hazelden.org

ISBN: 978-1-61649-679-1; ebook 978-1-61649-748-4

Library of Congress Cataloging-in-Publication Data is on file with the Library of Congress.

Editor's notes
In most cases, names, details, and circumstances have been changed to protect the privacy of those mentioned in this publication. When real names are given, it is with the person's permission.

This publication is not intended as a substitute for the advice of health care professionals.

21 20 19 18 17   1 2 3 4 5 6

Cover design by Terri Kinne
Interior design and typesetting by Hillspring Books, Inc.

To my ten-year-old self,
who learned that she was unlovable and unworthy of care

To my adult self,
who is disproving that idea by loving and caring for herself every day

And to every other person out there who can relate—because you, too,
are worthy of love and self-care

CONTENTS

Acknowledgments   ix

Introduction   xi

PART ONE
What Self-Care Is, What It Isn't, and Why You Aren't Doing It   1

CHAPTER ONE
What Self-Care Isn't   3

CHAPTER TWO
What Self-Care Is: Seven Guiding Principles   13

CHAPTER THREE
Three Kinds of Self-Care Magic (or, Even French Fries and Facebook Have Their Place)   21

PART TWO
Self-Evaluation   37

CHAPTER FOUR
You Are Here   39

PART THREE
The Magical Rewards of Self-Care   49

CHAPTER FIVE
Psychological and Emotional Self-Care   51

CHAPTER SIX
Self-Care and Your Body   71

CONTENTS

CHAPTER SEVEN

Caring for Yourself in Relationships: Partners, Family, Friends, and Others   83

CHAPTER EIGHT

The Beauty of Boundaries: Self-Care Skills for Relationships   97

CHAPTER NINE

Our Stuff, Ourselves: Self-Care and Our Belongings   119

CHAPTER TEN

Money Care Is Self-Care   133

CHAPTER ELEVEN

Self-Care at Work and Play   147

CHAPTER TWELVE

Self-Care and Your Spirit   167

Afterword   183

Notes   187

About the Author   191

ACKNOWLEDGMENTS

To my self-care teachers (in chronological order): Frances Martel, Charlotte Dubin, Karen Elizabeth Cohen, Wendy West Brenninkmeijer, Deborah Glatt Brautman, and Pamela Albro. Without each and every one of you, I couldn't have achieved the quality of self-care I've attained. Thank you for being my teachers.

Enormous thanks to Jennie Nash, Don Fehr, Mindy Keskinen, Sid Farrar, and Emily Reller: without you all, this book would be a vague and unrealized idea. And thank you to everyone who patiently endured my asking "So what do you do for self-care in this area of your life?" and generously answered my questions over and over again.

Thank you, Keith Dwyer, for your endless encouragement, support, patience, and love.

Introduction

WHEN WE THINK ABOUT SELF-CARE, we might think first of taking care of our physical being: fitness, beauty, keeping up appearances. Or we might think of dealing with stress, physical illness, or mental burnout—emergency care, as it were. Or maybe we imagine jumping on the latest self-help bandwagon, hoping that this one will make a difference.

The book in your hands aims to change all that. It's an invitation to see self-care as an attitude that permeates your life, a consistent self-replenishment. Self-care is a state of mind that offers a sense of abundance, a well that never runs dry. In this book we'll dig down to the depths of self-care—which is to say that this is a book about how to really and truly be an adult. I believe that the ability to do real self-care is one hallmark of adulthood, even though most adults are crappy at it.

When I was in graduate school twenty years ago, studying to become a therapist, many of my professors would occasionally mention the importance of self-care in our profession. "Being a therapist is hard, so be sure to do lots of self-care," the prof might say, and I'd create a heading in my notes and underline it—*Self-Care*—and then expectantly wait for the details. What was this vital and necessary thing that would allow me to do the work I wanted to do without getting drained and depleted?

But the secrets were never shared. Having duly noted the need for self-care, the professor would move on to the next topic, such as legal and ethical issues, and that "self-care" page of my notebook remained empty.

As I built my career over the next decade, I kept hearing the idea of self-care mentioned in professional settings: in conversations among therapists, in consultations, at conventions. And then the mainstream media picked it up, and the topic expanded outward: self-care was seen as critical not just for health care professionals, but for all of us. "Life is hard, so be sure to do lots of self-care," the women's magazines cooed (or screamed)—but just like my professors, they never outlined the steps, the details, that would assure me I was doing this ongoing self-care thing *right*. We were all supposed to take time for ourselves in order to deal with stress, achieve balance, be better parents, better workers, and better mates. A good, solid concept. But where was the how-to? The self-care advice and examples always seemed simplistic and superficial: *Keep a journal. Take a yoga class. Light a candle.*

Lovely ideas. But really, how impactful is that candle in the face of a life filled with the daily ordinary and extraordinary challenges and stresses that we all endure? (Years later, a friend griped to me, "Self-care is more than a stupid candle!")

Herbal teas, massages, pedicures . . . and, more recently, memory improvement apps and meditation podcasts—all of these promise to ease our stress, tame our tensions, or widen our bandwidth, but in the long run, they don't— not really. Used on their own, they're the equivalent of self-care Band-Aids: they hold us together and treat the pain for now, but they don't get to the heart of the matter.

Now don't get me wrong: there's a place in our lives for these things. But when we treat ourselves with these small indulgences as an attempt at primary self-care, we might as well be saying, "I deserve this day at the spa (*or this night out with the girls / Dove dark chocolate bar / new phone / pretty dress / scented candle . . .*) because I am burned out and poorly taken care of. So, to postpone caring for myself in the really critical areas, I am giving myself this little treat."

Looking around at the array of treats, I knew there had to be more to it. Was there some secret society of self-care practitioners who could enlighten me if only I could figure out the secret handshake? Where did they meet? I wanted to find them and ask so many questions. What does self-care really mean? Where do I start? How do I change the habits of a lifetime? How do I maintain my progress? And how, exactly, does self-care ease the difficulty of being a therapist charged with helping people through trauma, heartbreak, and hopelessness?

When I started my own therapy practice, my understanding of self-care got a lot more practical, because I could feel the impact of my work on my mind, body, and spirit. If I didn't eat well, sleep well, or take regular breaks, I burned out, melted down, and had a hissy fit or three. I began to see that to do a good job for my clients, I *needed* to really care for myself.

Soon I was mentoring interns in self-care and reminding my clients about it, too. But even as I did, I wasn't fully practicing what I was preaching. You see, I am not naturally good at self-care. I hate to admit it, but I've been lousy at it at times, coming as I do from a family that neither modeled self-care nor taught me its value.

I've always tended to neglect my needs, even well into adulthood. Once, during a period of exceptionally bad self-care, a friend suggested that if I were treating a child the way I was treating myself, I would likely lose custody. I knew she was right, and I was mortified. I was depriving myself of sleep, rest, healthy food, even water. I took no time to care for my home or my body because, as I saw it, I simply didn't have time. No time to grab a sweater if I was cold or a snack if I was hungry. A doctor when I was sick? No time. So, as you can see, my own education in true self-care was difficult and took a long time. But eventually I got there—and, as for everyone, it is an ongoing work in progress. As our needs change, we must adapt our self-care practices to fit our current reality.

So I am writing this book in the time-honored tradition of "You teach what you had to learn yourself—the hard way." But that's why I may be just the person to write this book. I am not going to stand on the self-care mountaintop and tell you to do what I do. I'll be honest with you. I'll tell you where I still suck, where I used to suck but got better, and, most important, what we can *both* do to get better at this thing called self-care.

• • •

Why is it so hard? If self-care is so clearly in our own interest, why aren't we already doing it? Many people have a lot of resistance to self-care, and for reasons rarely discussed in the literature on the subject. Many are reasons we aren't always aware of ourselves: guilt, shame, a sense of inadequacy and low self-worth, self-sabotage, self-harm, family-of-origin issues (modeling our parents' treatment of themselves or us), depression, masochism, victim mentality, a too-stringent work ethic, a refusal to grow up (including an infantile desire to be taken care of by other people)—the list goes on.

And what about the claim—or the unquestioned belief—that self-care is selfish? If nothing else, this book will challenge that claim. It is baloney, BS, hooey, hogwash, and balderdash that self-care is selfish. You may know this, deep down. We can't give when we have nothing to give. We all know the drill: the airline attendant reminds us that, should we need to use an oxygen mask, "Secure your own mask first before assisting others." What we learn here is that we can't take care of others before we take care of ourselves.

The subtext of that narrative, however, is that we wouldn't need self-preservation for any other reason than to be able to take care of other people. It's as if we're all supposed to be totally selfless, and other people's needs are the only way to justify self-care. Is someone else is in dire straits? Then I'd better make sure I can show up for them. In this book, we will challenge that notion.

Sheer survival isn't selfish; doing a better job of caring for yourself isn't either—it's just common sense. Let me underscore this: if you're worried about selfishness, it is absolutely *more* selfish to *not* do self-care than to do it. If you don't do it, there will be consequences for your health, happiness, relationships, and longevity. If you don't take care of yourself, someone else is going to have to take care of you, making it indeed selfish to not practice self-care to begin with.

And *with* self-care, we might just reach a level of clarity and creativity that we've dreamed of but never thought we'd attain. In taking care of ourselves, we move into becoming real adults. We may be breaking a whole lot of rules we learned from family, society, and even our religion, but we become real and self-actualized adults. Through taking extraordinary care of ourselves, we may be choosing to treat ourselves differently than we've been treated by others. We're saying that we are important and worthy of being treated well—and that may take extra effort if we're still overcoming some past trauma or difficulty. We all need to learn how to love ourselves, and self-care is often the first step.

Because sometimes the action has to come first. Doing self-care is a way of saying that we matter. And when we start to *treat* ourselves like we matter, we start to actually believe that we really *do* matter. And others see it, too. The more we take care of ourselves, the less likely we are to tolerate bad behavior, abuse, and disrespect from others. Self-care is not an add-on, not something you have to schedule, but rather a central part of how to live a life.

In this book, we'll explore self-care in many areas of life—including body, mind and emotions, spirit, relationships, finances, material possessions, work, and play. We'll look at the challenges people tend to have in each area and how to address those needs from the inside out. As we do so, we'll be applying seven key principles of self-care: rules of thumb you can use every day to up your quality of life. We'll also take a playful look at three kinds of "magic"— the self-care strategies we might already be using. As you'll see, these strategies range from the wholesome to the dangerous, with a broad and fascinating territory in between.

You'll hear some other viewpoints in this book, too. You'll meet some of today's experts and researchers in the self-care field, and you'll meet (or re-meet) psychologist Abraham Maslow, whose "hierarchy of needs" gives us a useful self-care template. You'll also hear from some everyday people from various walks of life—people who generously shared their self-care stories with me. Some responded to an online survey; others I exchanged views with more informally. Where real names are given, it is with the person's permission.

As a therapist, I've guided many clients who were surprised to trace some of their problems to poor self-care. And I've been thrilled and honored to see how their lives were transformed when they took steps to care for themselves and their relationships with more integrity. You'll meet some of them in this book. I've changed (or omitted) names and also changed personal details so they are unrecognizable. But the power of their stories is true to life.

●　　●　　●

So this book is your invitation to self-care. I request the pleasure of your company. And let's think about that phrase "RSVP" for a moment—*Répondez, s'il vous plaît*, or "Please respond." In this book, we're learning to practice self-care by *responding* to our true selves. Not *reacting* to our stresses, our cravings, our burnout. Responding. When we pay attention to ourselves every day, we can respond to our deepest needs over the long term. We invest in ourselves, and that investment yields wonderful rewards.

None of us is perfect at self-care, and we can all improve. If nothing else, I hope this book shows you that self-care is about loving yourself, warts and all, and that you are more than worthy of that love.

Welcome.

 Self-love is a prerequisite for the abundant life you've always dreamed of.

PART ONE

What Self-Care Is, What It Isn't, and Why You Aren't Doing It

The Golden Rule is "Do unto others as you would have them do unto you."
The Platinum Rule is "How I treat myself is training others how to treat me."

—Michael Bernard Beckwith, minister and founder of the Agape International Spiritual Center

I get to work before the sun comes up and I leave long after it's gone down.
I haven't had sex in six months with someone other than myself.
And the only thing in my refrigerator is an old lime. Could be a kiwi,
no way to tell. But here's the thing, this is just temporary.

—Nick Hendricks, character in the movie *Horrible Bosses*

CHAPTER ONE

What Self-Care Isn't

SELF-CARE: WHAT IS IT? It's a tricky term to define because our culture perpetuates a dizzying array of misconceptions about it. So let's start with those. Let's first disabuse ourselves of the notions that may be mucking up our ability to take care of ourselves. Let's start with what self-care *isn't*.

Self-Care Myths We May Believe without Knowing It

So we're going to start by exploring those misbeliefs and debunking each one. I've identified seven. Let's start with the simple misconceptions and work up to the more diabolical ones—the often-unconscious beliefs that can subtly but surely undermine our self-care skills.

Myth: Self-care is just for mothers, health care providers, and other caregivers.

Our culture tends to focus self-care discussions on individuals who spend the bulk of their time in the *business* of caregiving. It's not a big topical leap to look at how those people are caring for *themselves*—because if they're doing a lousy job of it, then they will fail at their primary task of caring for others, whether they're providing health care, raising children, or caring for aging adults. But to limit the discussion to caregivers is very shortsighted. All of us, in all walks of life, are in the self-care business, even if we aren't doing a very good job at it.

Myth: Self-care is a section of Whole Foods where you buy essential oils and scented candles.

For many of us, the term *self-care* might mean purchasing and consuming frivolous feel-good items, going on shopping sprees, or spending an afternoon at a spa, gym, or yoga class. We might also think of escaping by binge-watching a TV series, eating a pint of ice cream in one sitting, or reading a trashy novel. And yes, occasionally, these could all have a place in our self-care repertoire. The question is, are we doing them routinely? Do we turn to them in reaction to built-up stress, as a "reward" for getting through a difficult day, or as an impulsive response to media triggers? Or are they periodic indulgences and treats that we incorporate into a well-thought-out, meaningful self-care plan—a plan built around daily attention to our emotional, mental, physical, and spiritual health?

Myth: Self-care is just self-soothing.

Self-care is often equated with seeking sensual pleasure, such as bathing with special oils, getting a massage, or having sex, whether with another person or alone (and let's throw in the scented candle, while we're at it!). As with the other things we do to reward ourselves or ease stress, soothing yourself can be temporary self-indulgent escapism, or it can be a natural, healthy, enjoyable part of an ongoing self-care plan.

Myth: Self-care is for people who have nothing else to do.

I hear this excuse pretty much every day: "I know I should exercise, sleep more, and not get my dinner from the drive-thru, but there just isn't time." Yes, I get it; there are only twenty-four hours in a day. I know you work fifty, or eighty, hours a week and you have to sleep. But you *are* sleeping, bathing, and eating. You have a domicile of some sort, and you have some ongoing relationships with people—and each of those is an area where you can be doing better self-care. Quantity of time may be limited, but you can always up the quality. It's not about perfection; it's about taking care of yourself as well as possible so you can do all that you want to do. We will see that setting up your life so that you *never* have time to take care of yourself is going to come with deep consequences.

Myth: Self-care is just for the rich and privileged.

Do you think of self-care as the self-indulgence of the elite and wealthy—the luxurious spa resorts that come with fresh, customized healthy cuisine, one-on-one meditation and yoga practices, and aromatherapy massages? Forget it. Effective self-care isn't a function of how much money you have—it's a mind-set. It takes no money to go on a walk, relax and read a library book, visit a friend, or literally stop and smell the roses.

Are you with me so far? Good. Now let's turn to the two biggest misconceptions about self-care. These two rear their ugly heads everywhere, all the time.

Myth: Self-care is selfish.

I often hear people claim that doing self-care would make them feel "selfish." One dictionary defines *selfish* as "concerned excessively or exclusively with oneself without regard for others." Self-care is not about excessive concern for self; it is about taking good enough care of yourself so that you can function, be productive, be in healthy relationships, and have the ability and energy to be there for others you care about. A narcissist, the poster child for selfishness, would believe that they are the *only* one in the entire world who should be cared for and demands that others abandon their own needs to care for them. Unlike narcissists, we're not expecting those we love to take crappy care of themselves in order to serve us better. I've never heard a client say, "You know, I wish my kid (or spouse, or parent) would stop with all the self-care and put that energy into caring for me." But when it comes time to take care of *ourselves,* we often imagine that everyone has a different expectation for us than we do for them.

The truth is that if we are sick, exhausted, overworked, overwhelmed, resentful, and angry, we can't be present for those we love. If we have nothing inside ourselves, how much do we have to give? I will answer that for you: bupkes, nada, and diddly-squat. By taking care of ourselves, we have more energy, health, love, chi, and mojo to give to others. We can live a life that is productive, generative, and of service to those we love and care for.

Myth: Self-care is a sin.

Our country was founded by Protestant Christians. My guess is that whatever our actual religion, most of us have absorbed some version of the Protestant work ethic, which states that hard work is pretty much the only thing worthy of reward and praise, either here on earth or in heaven. The Bible-rooted proverb "Idle hands are the devil's workshop" is in our cultural DNA. The American dream is a version of this belief: work relentlessly hard, never give up, and you will win.

It's heavy stuff. I see patients every day who are working themselves to the bone in the name of a god they may or may not even believe in—because they think that *not* doing so is not only selfish but also immoral and sinful. Most of us have been programmed to believe that hard work and self-sacrifice make us morally superior and that slowing down and taking care of ourselves would somehow compromise us.

Rabbi and author Lev Baesh would disagree with that. He says, "Teaching Torah is about teaching right behavior. It includes self-care [as well as] the care of others, care of the planet, care of our historical stories and struggles, and care of future generations."[1]

Many other spiritual leaders say the same thing. Televangelist Joyce Meyer, for example, makes self-care a high priority in her ministry.

"I found out something very valuable to me: I cannot give away what I don't have," she says. "If I don't love myself, I can't love you. If I am not peaceful I can't bring peace into your life. If I have no joy, how can I give you joy? You have to spend some time loving yourself. And that doesn't mean to be in love *with* yourself. It means to respect yourself enough to take care of yourself. I take care of myself . . . in a way that I believe brings glory to God [by keeping] me strong and healthy."[2]

What We Might Do Instead of Self-Care

Self-care is not just up against these cultural misunderstandings. It is also up against powerful internal forces—potent habits we all tend to adopt *instead* of self-care. Let's take a brief look at them, so we can continue to understand the landscape of self-care.

Self-neglect

Barbara, a psychotherapist friend, describes her lack of self-care as *self-neglect*. She says, "It's really about intention for me. If I do not intentionally prioritize myself, I fall into self-neglect. For me it doesn't feel malicious or intentionally sabotaging (although that might have been the case for me many years ago), but *neglect* definitely fits."

The dictionary definition of *neglect* is "lack of attention or care that someone or something needs." That says it all. Are you neglecting your body, mind, spirit, finances, possessions, relationships, and boundaries in big or small ways? Which aspects of yourself are you not paying adequate attention to? No one has every area of their life completely together. Every one of us has at least one area we're neglecting at any given time.

Here's an example: at one point, I was neglecting my body by sitting for too many hours at a stretch at work. Finally, my back decided it would scream and yell and demand I do something differently. Still, I had to motivate myself by committing to it financially and actually scheduling times to take care of my neglected spine. I reluctantly hired a trainer to develop some exercises I could use to address the problem. It helped, and as you'd expect, this trainer guy took incredible care of his own body. And yet, this same guy admitted that he never had time to see friends or socialize. That confirmed for me that all of us have areas where we wouldn't dream of neglecting ourselves, but we also have other areas where we do such a bad job that we should be fired from being the boss of these domains.

Self-sabotage

The opposite of self-care is to behave in ways that undermine our goals for personal well-being. This kind of non-self-care can be tricky to identify, because we often do it unconsciously and even passive-aggressively. Look at how you care for yourself: can you see any ways you are actually setting yourself up for suffering? Self-sabotage often masquerades as martyrdom: we care for others to the detriment of caring for ourselves. Or we don't prioritize our own emotional and physical health because we assume we'll fail or that we don't deserve the rewards of self-care. Often the lie of self-sabotage is, *It doesn't matter if I do something good for myself; I'm not worth it and it probably won't make a difference anyway.* We make it an either-or decision. We adopt an all-or-nothing mind-set that assumes the only choice is between self-care and self-neglect. Choosing the latter only confirms our sense of failure.

Beth, a hardworking corporate marketing executive, describes her own tendencies in this area:

> My self-sabotage is seated in the "You're not good enough or worthy of this" center of my mind. I usually catch it when I find myself thinking that there's no point in doing X because I won't achieve Y, whether that's exercising to lose weight, applying for a job I want, or pursuing a business opportunity to attain more financial freedom. I think, *You're not good enough, so why even try?*
>
> With that attitude, I start eating junk food and telling myself, "Screw it—you only live once!" . . . Or I don't submit my résumé for a job I mostly qualify for because I don't have *all* the ideal qualifications listed (never mind that those are usually recruiters' wish lists, and less qualified people get hired for jobs all the time). . . . Or I mull over a business idea in my mind for ages only to find that someone beat me to the punch. My self-sabotage likes all-or-nothing terms. Either I'm going hard in the gym, eating all the protein and veggies, applying for all the jobs, hashing out all the business ideas, styling all the badass outfits—*or* I'm eating crap, not going to the gym, not applying for any jobs, setting aside business ideas, and wearing the same boring outfit on repeat.

Now that Beth is aware of this tendency, she can start catching herself and find a sustainable happy medium.

Self-betrayal

Self-betrayal, unlike self-sabotage, is usually conscious from the get-go. With this kind of non-self-care, we tell ourselves, "I know this is a priority, and even so, I'm not doing it." Self-betrayal comes in many forms. We choose to eat the food we know will make us feel crappy, we accept a work assignment when we're already maxed out, we take on an unwise financial obligation, we ignore the calendar's alert to schedule that mammogram or colonoscopy. When we choose to ignore what we know is the right choice, we're not just acting in an un-self-caring way; we are betraying ourselves. We try to let ourselves off the hook by saying, "I know it would be good for me to see the doctor (or take the day off, or get some rest, or say no to this request), but I can't because . . ." (add your favorite excuse here). But really, if we owned the truth, we'd say, "I am actively betraying myself by making this choice." Then we'd have a chance to change that habit. It's harder to make a detrimental choice if we admit we're aware of the consequences at some level.

Monica, a busy mother and graduate student, still struggles with that awareness. "I know exactly what I need to do, and when it comes time to make the choice, I almost always opt out," she says. "I tell myself it doesn't matter; I'll do it later. It looks like procrastination or laziness, but I know that in truth I am betraying myself."

Self-betrayal may be rooted in other non-self-caring motives, such as feelings of self-hate or a mind-set of self-neglect. Or maybe we think our worth comes solely through achievement and work. Or it may simply be that we are continuing to care for ourselves in the negative ways others have cared for us in the past.

Self-sacrifice

This version of non-self-care has some pride to it. People say, "I am not taking care of myself because I am selfless, and I care more about others than myself." Self-sacrificers may even brag to others about their lack of self-care, enjoying the ego hits from their self-image: how giving, loving, and wonderful they are for driving themselves into the ground doing good works for others, or putting their career first, or whatever it is they are sacrificing for. Self-sacrifice is intentional. We say, "I am choosing not to give myself care," with the core assumption being *it is good and noble for me to suffer.*

But please hear me on this: no matter how worthy the cause—and there are many worthy causes—if your body, your finances, your emotional health, and your general well-being are continually depleted, you will eventually have an empty well. It comes down to a simple economic truth: if you are bankrupt, you can't give to others.

Elaine, an English teacher, notices her habit of putting others' needs ahead of her own. "I've always felt that I, and my needs, are not important enough to merit self-care," she says. But that habit is shifting. "I have come to the realization that not taking care of myself is almost akin to denying my existence and my right to have my needs met. It's a lack of self-validation. It even, in a certain way, allows me to put myself in a victim mode, which in a lot of ways is easier than validating myself, which requires me to face difficult truths."

Self-hatred

Related to self-sabotage, but more blatant and ingrained, self-hatred sends this message: "Since I don't like myself, I don't deserve to be taken care of." It manifests in other internal messages as well, like "It just doesn't matter if I do it or I don't; I'm not worth doing anything for. None of it makes a difference anyway." Like the other motivators of non-self-care, self-hatred stems from the past: we likely absorbed these negative feelings about ourselves as we were growing up. When key people in our lives communicated that we don't matter, we took those messages to heart.

I'm not telling you that self-care will heal all your childhood wounds, that it will instantly fill that hole where feelings of adequacy, worth, and lovability belong. But establishing the habit of self-care can have an impact by transforming your internal negative self-talk into positive self-talk, which translates into the bigger message *I matter.* If you are wounded, your self-care practice might at first feel like just a task without a purpose. But consistent self-care can change self-hate to the belief that we are worthy of love.

Self-harm

In the case of active self-punishment, professional help is called for. But the same is true for extreme, long-term self-neglect. When we hear the term *self-harm,* we often think of self-injurious behaviors like self-mutilation and cutting. We might also think of suicide. But self-harm can also come from cumulative effects. Long-term self-neglect can have an impact on our bodies, our health, and our well-being that is extremely self-injurious. A persistent lack of self-care can be purposeful and intentionally cruel—even suicidal in its underlying intent.

Underneath this dramatic lack of self-care is a whole lot of pain that requires more attention than the self-care strategies we're talking about in this book can provide. Professional help is needed here. For chronic self-neglect or active self-punishment, please seek professional help from a psychiatrist or therapist. If you're not sure where to start, ask a doctor or social worker. Or check a reputable "Find a Therapist" web page like those at Psychology Today (https://therapists.psychologytoday.com) or Theravive (www.theravive.com).

· · ·

So these are the habits we might adopt *instead of* self-care. If you recognize yourself in any of these tendencies, welcome to the human race. Whatever your justifications for not caring for yourself, you've got lots of company.

And welcome, too, to the self-care approaches you'll find in this book. In the end, I believe the answer to overcoming our barriers to practicing self-care is, simply, learning to love ourselves. That may sound like a huge task—like I am asking you to come up with the cure for cancer or the way to end world hunger—but this is doable. You can do this, I promise.

Now let's look at seven principles that can help us express self-love in action.

 If we have nothing inside ourselves, how much do we have to give? Bupkes, nada, and diddly-squat.

CHAPTER TWO

What Self-Care Is

Seven Guiding Principles

MOST OF US ARE PRETTY CLEAR on what it means to take care of people we love, but we're foggier on what it means to take care of ourselves. As I started to think deeply about this subject, I asked lots of people—both formally and informally—what the term *self-care* meant to them. A woman answering that question typically started by lambasting herself: she knew she wasn't doing much self-care, she should do a better job, and here's what she intended to do as soon as she could manage the time. But when I asked a man, he often seemed to draw a complete blank. Of course, as I questioned both women and men further, I got some deeper responses (and stories), and you'll find some of them in this book. But whether you *know* you aren't doing a great job with self-care, or you're not even sure what self-care means, you've picked up this book to figure it out. So congratulations: you have decided that you are important enough to make self-care an integral part of your life.

You may not have paused to ask yourself what self-care is or how to do it well. But there are probably some people in your life whom you love like crazy, and you may have some opinions on how they could up *their* game on the self-care front. I bet if I asked you to, you could come up with a detailed report. Here are some possible examples:

- Your husband won't go to the doctor or take time to exercise.
- Your best friend is in a relationship with a total jerk who treats her so badly, you'd like to break up with him for her.
- Your sister's house, car, and finances are in chronic disrepair, and she could easily be featured on *Hoarders*.

- Your daughter won't eat her fruits or vegetables, and you fear that the school nurse is going to inform you she has scurvy.

- Your adolescent son bathes so infrequently that you've considered installing ceiling showers over his bed so you could spray him clean, along with his pigsty of a room, from time to time.

Now that you've begun your own mental list of what the people in your life are doing wrong, go ahead and write it all down in glorious detail. Then add what you think they *should* be doing. I did this exercise myself, and it was a great list—very astute, if I do say so myself. But after I wrote my list, I did what I am now going to ask you to do with yours: crumple it up and throw it in the trash.

I know—it's disappointing, right? Well, the sad truth is that there's nothing you can do to get others to care for themselves, especially in the ways *you* think would be best. Okay, you do need to motivate your kids, and maybe your spouse or partner now and then, but there are limits even there.

But here's the good news: you can use all that critical ability on someone you *can* have some impact on—you, dear you. *You* have some locus of control over *you*. You can actually improve your self-care, right here and now.

Let's Get Real: Seven Principles for Self-Care Practice

Here are your touchstones: seven principles to help you discover the self-care practices that are effective, adaptable, and sustainable for you.

Principle 1: Self-care is a daily, lifelong practice.

Self-care is something you do every day, consciously or not. Your eating habits are, for better or worse, a form of self-care, as are your sleep habits, your exercise habits, the condition of your home, and the way you conduct yourself at work. If you are alive, you're engaging in some form of self-care—whether you're doing a good, fair, or poor job of it. All those daily activities can be done in a way that is either nourishing or depleting.

Take sleep, for example. Does your bed comfort and support you? Is your bedding clean? Are you getting by with the skimpy pillows you've had since you were a kid? Do you sleep with your phone next to your head, letting it torment you with a ping for every new message? What kind of alarm do you have to start your day—a caustic clang, or a gentle and Zen-like alert? Do you hit the snooze button so many times that your morning becomes a hectic game of catch-up? Sleep is just one of the daily self-care activities that you may be underestimating as a factor in your well-being.

When I have a choice to make, I've learned to ask myself, "Is this action, activity, or decision going to deplete me or energize me?" Just being aware is one of my major self-care practices.

Principle 2: Self-care is self-love.

Self-love is the simple act of caring for yourself as you would care for anyone you really and truly loved. How would you treat yourself if you were the person you respected and cared about the most? Well, engaging in self-care is doing just that. And remember, sometimes the action precedes the feeling. Starting a new self-care habit can actually improve our self-concept and self-worth, and boost our sense of being worthy of love. Whenever I take the time to treat myself with love and attention—instead of blowing off my needs for the sake of expediency or because I don't feel worthy—I am saying that I matter.

Principle 3: Self-care means taking personal responsibility.

You may be responsible for all kinds of jobs, tasks, and people, but ultimately what you are really and truly responsible for is your own well-being. If you're over eighteen and are of fundamentally sound mind and body, you are legally not dependent on others for your care, even if you might still be financially or emotionally. You might be a write-off on someone else's taxes. You might have some dependency issues to clean up. But at the end of the day, you have many kinds of personal adult responsibilities that are yours and yours alone. This is your body, this is your life, and it is up to you how will you take care of it or not take care of it. The consequences of those choices—good or bad—are primarily on you, even taking into account the inevitable repercussions for the other people in your life. No one can do a crappy job of self-care and not pay the piper. Maybe someone will pay your bills, right some wrongs for you, or clean up some of your messes. But at the end of the day, the costs of shortchanging your body, mind, soul, home, belongings, and relationships fall mainly on you. Your quality of life, your satisfaction, your fulfillment.

I recently bought a new car—my first nice car that was brand new and intended just for me. Until now, I've always inherited cars in one way or another, and to be super honest, I didn't care if they lasted long or not. I didn't consciously *know* that fact; my indifference about the cars just showed up in my somewhat neglectful behavior. But when I got my new car, my whole attitude changed. I keep my car clean inside and out, and I take it for regular washes and oil changes. I know my maintenance schedule. I avoid parking where the doors might get dinged. Why do I go to all this trouble? I care about the car and I want it to last. I know that if I don't do these things, my shiny new car will turn into a beater. And I hate to admit it, but over the years, in some ways I have treated *myself* like a 1989 beater car that I use as a personal trashcan and not a classy vehicle that I really care about. Do you have cherished possessions? How do you care for them? Self-care is taking personal responsibility for yourself in the same way.

Principle 4: Self-care means noticing what matters to us.
You can tell a lot about a person by what they tend to the most. In my life, my relationship with my life partner, my work, and my dog all get an awful lot of care. I have, on many occasions, sacrificed my own care and happiness for them. Let me give you an example. My beloved West Highland White Terrier, Lily, enjoys the kind of care that many people will never know. Lily is spoiled, and I know it. I hesitate to share with you the degree to which she is spoiled, but I do so in order to make a point: Lily may be better cared for than I am. Let's call this an object lesson. My own priorities are revealed all too clearly when I notice my behavior toward Lily.

Lily has a diet of organic dog food. And while I'm just fine if my fridge is empty, if Lily needs more food, I will gladly make an emergency run to the local pet food store rather than give her something not on her regular menu. If Lily has a little boo-boo on her precious face, I will not be able to control my anxiety: I'll take her to the vet ASAP. Meanwhile, I might put off scheduling my colonoscopy or even picking up the prescriptions waiting for me at the pharmacy.

There's no mistaking that Lily matters a whole lot to me. What's important for me to notice is how and why caring for Lily matters so much. What's behind it? What does that suggest about where my other priorities lie—including my own self-care? Is a change in order? There's no one right answer; we all need to answer such questions for ourselves.

Principle 5: Self-care requires attention and responsiveness.
Self-care isn't just taking good enough care of ourselves to get by. It's about *attending* to what we actually need and *responding* to those needs, through long-term or short-term action. Rather than thinking of self-care as a structured plan that you administer by rote, try thinking of it as *responsive*. What do I mean by "responsive"? It's what we do to respond to whatever our awareness indicates are real needs. We can view self-care as responsive self-parenting, rather than that "scheduled feeding" kind of parenting. Scheduled feedings are great, in theory, but they don't always work out, right? Feeding habits evolve. Your needs do, too. With *real* self-care, it's not enough to say, "I will do this good thing for myself every day at this time, and it is not up for negotiation." As with any relationship, care of self often requires that we check in on ourselves to see what's required in the moment, then make the mindful effort to do it well.

It can be difficult to "take our temperature" and ask ourselves about the basics of our physical health (diet, exercise, and sleep), let alone assess what we need in more nuanced areas of our lives: relationship boundaries, spiritual comfort, or fun and play, for example. Most of my conscious attention, as demonstrated by my to-do list, is about self-care as I set priorities in my work life. While writing this passage, for example, I just did a check-in and noticed I felt low energy. Now, it would be ideal if I could respond to that by going for a walk or maybe taking a nap. But the truth is that I don't have time for either of those if I want to avoid the stress of missing my writing deadline—so I determined that what I needed was some coffee. Is that self-care, or is that like giving a pacifier to a crying baby? Sometimes a pacifier (and coffee) can be self-care. But let's also hope that my awareness of low energy will guide how I proceed for the rest of the day. Update: Soon after my coffee break, my fiancé, Keith, asked if I wanted to go to a movie later. And although that sounds like fun, the truth is that I'll need to go to bed early tonight to restore my energy. For me, self-care means knowing this and saying no to a nice evening out with Keith.

Principle 6: Self-care must be realistic to be effective.

To engage in self-care is to admit that you are a human being with limited energy and resources, and a fragile body that has an expiration date. Up to a point we may be able to neglect ourselves and pretend that we don't need to be cared for, that we are above it. The reality is that there's a basic level of self-care we can't ignore: to survive, we all need water, food, sleep, shelter from the elements, and some basic connection with other people. And as we'll see in principle 7, we have other needs that go beyond mere survival if we are to be fulfilled as human beings. We may pretend we can burn our candle at both ends and cut ourselves off from others without consequences. But denial does not protect us from this reality: if we're not serious about self-care, we will never know what it is to be our best selves. Ultimately, self-care is key to self-fulfillment.

Principle 7: Self-care precedes self-fulfillment.

Before I went to school to become a therapist, my bookcases were filled with row after row of how-to books—how to deal with various emotional disorders, improve relationships, succeed in life, win friends and influence people, unleash my power within—and in none of those books did I find any guidance on what self-care really means at a deep level. Finally, in grad school I discovered an author who wrote seriously about self-care, only at the time I didn't realize that was his true subject. I just thought it was another therapy model I had to memorize to pass a test. That author was Abraham Maslow, a psychologist who was interested in what motivates people.

His theory, known as the hierarchy of needs, holds that all human beings meet their needs in a particular order. Our most basic physiological demands must be satisfied before we are free to focus on our needs for safety and security. With those needs met, we can then strive for love and belonging, then for esteem. Finally, we can work toward self-actualization, which Maslow defined as "the desire for self-fulfillment . . . the desire to become more and more what one is, to become everything that one is capable of becoming."[3] Self-actualization is theoretically possible for everyone, but the underlying needs must be fulfilled for self-actualization to ever occur.

I had read Maslow, I knew his theory, and yet for years I lived in exact opposition to it. Essentially, I believed that someday, after years of self-denial,

I would earn the right and acquire the ability to finally take care of myself, to be good to me. Turns out I had it "bass-ackwards," as my mother used to say. My plan was in essence to restrict, deny, and self-abandon my way to self-actualization. Only—surprise, surprise—it never worked. I would set a goal in my work life or my personal life and pour myself 100 percent into achieving it, abandoning my other needs completely—and would then feel drained, exhausted, and depressed. To compensate for my self-neglect, I would tell myself I deserved a treat: food, lipstick, hours of watching crap TV, then sleeping late, or whatever might give me some of what I thought Maslow was saying I needed. (Okay, he never said anything about lipstick or TV, but he did mention food, water, and sleep.)

So, let's take a look at Maslow's hierarchy of needs as a pyramid. Our human needs are shown here in the order Maslow says we must achieve them, with our most basic ones at the bottom.

MASLOW'S HIERARCHY OF NEEDS[4]

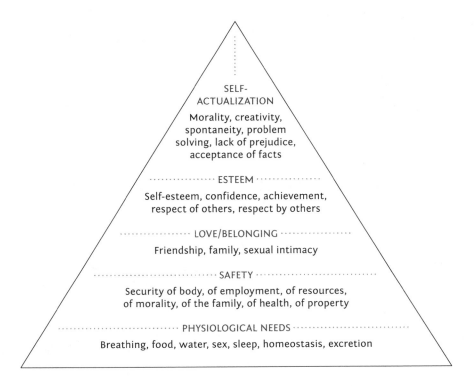

SELF-ACTUALIZATION
Morality, creativity, spontaneity, problem solving, lack of prejudice, acceptance of facts

ESTEEM
Self-esteem, confidence, achievement, respect of others, respect by others

LOVE/BELONGING
Friendship, family, sexual intimacy

SAFETY
Security of body, of employment, of resources, of morality, of the family, of health, of property

PHYSIOLOGICAL NEEDS
Breathing, food, water, sex, sleep, homeostasis, excretion

I believe that when we practice real self-care to meet each level of need, each of us has the potential to reach our own personal pinnacle of self-actualization— to feel fulfilled and be the best person we can be.

. . .

Let these seven principles be your guideposts as you examine your own self-care practices: as they are now, and as you want them to be. We'll refer to them often in this book.

In the next chapter, we'll see how healthy, sustainable self-care can be achieved through lots of types of practices. Even some that might look or feel self-indulgent can have their place in an effective, ongoing self-care plan.

 Treat yourself like the person you respect and care about the most.

Three Kinds of Self-Care Magic

(or, Even French Fries and Facebook Have Their Place)

The problem with people who have no vices is that . . .
they're going to have some pretty annoying virtues.

—Elizabeth Taylor

NOW THAT YOU KNOW how important self-care is, what it is, and what it isn't, it should be super simple to define what self-care looks like—or so you'd think. But self-care isn't that simple. It's subjective, slippery, and context dependent. It's more of a postmodern potpourri than an Old Testament Ten Commandments kind of deal.

True, there are some self-care activities that are just objectively good: healthy diet and exercise, for example. And there are other splurge-type activities that have some clear dangers, say, frequent nights at the casino. These are short-term substitutes for real self-care, and later, they leave us feeling more depleted and less cared for than if we hadn't done them at all.

But other kinds of self-care activities can *look* to the casual observer like either self-neglect or self-indulgence when in fact they are not. (For example, a working mom might decide to skip her Zumba class and watch YouTube makeup tutorials for an hour instead. The fact is, there are days when watching someone do a perfect winged eyeliner will truly be more refreshing for her.) And still other self-care activities—the guilty pleasures—might even embarrass us, and yet they can actually be nurturing, kind, and supportive in the right context. If we *never* get an evening of french fries and Facebook, is life really worth living? I think you can guess my answer.

When we reflect on those three examples, we see that context is key. Self-care relies on self-knowledge and the ability to check in with ourselves to see what we truly need *at a given time.* I can't offer you a self-care list of do's and don'ts. But, as illustrated by those three examples, what I can offer you is a way to evaluate your current self-care activities and perhaps begin to allow more self-care into your everyday life.

It comes down to three kinds of magic. Yes, I'm borrowing from language that seems like it belongs more in Hogwarts and Harry Potter than in a self-help book, but please consider it shorthand, rather than evidence that self-care is a form of witchcraft. The magic I'm talking about is not the occult kind. Rather, it's a wonderful, surprising, and almost miraculous method of change. But to stick with the metaphor of the occult, White Magic is considered good or benign—the kind of spell a "good witch" might cast—while Black Magic is considered dark and destructive.

So how does that apply to self-care? Well, White Magic self-care is the wholesome stuff: good sleep, diet, and exercise, for example. Black Magic self-care habits are the dangerous ones, the playing-with-fire habits like substance abuse or compulsive gambling, and they are the kind that are never, ever good for us. And Gray Magic self-care? Gray Magic shows us that, in fact, there's a middle ground. These choices are all on a spectrum. When we consciously make a less-than-wholesome choice, that's fine, occasionally. It might be a splurge, an exception to our rule, giving us an enjoyable kick. Let's call that Gray Magic. But if it starts becoming a habit, we're headed for Black Magic territory.

And speaking of language, it's unfortunate that, in English, *white* connotes positive while *black* connotes negative. That duality is embedded in so many of our words and phrases: "white lie" and "dark arts," for example. I use the terms White Magic and Black Magic simply as a convenience, with zero social commentary intended.

Let's take a closer look at these three types of magic.

THREE KINDS OF SELF-CARE MAGIC

White Magic Self-Care

As I said previously, White Magic is the use of supernatural powers for good or selfless ends. White Magic self-care, while not supernatural, employs our own powers for the self-care actions that we'd all agree are good for us. None of us would question the wisdom of saving for a rainy day, flossing, taking your vitamins, eating leafy greens, wearing galoshes when it rains, engaging in safe sex, and getting eight hours of sleep a night. But we may have differing ideas on what these actions actually *look like* in practice. After all, one person's belief in juice fasting as basic self-care would scare the poop out of others.

As noted earlier, many people imagine self-care as calming and soothing—activities like baths, meditation, and relaxation exercises. But for other people, self-care might include heavy metal music, rock climbing, political involvement, poetry slams, or martial arts. For some folks, hitting a punching bag is more self-fulfilling than getting a two-hour massage.

So White Magic self-care may look different to you than it does to your neighbor. What is White Magic self-care for some can also be abused and twisted in a way that causes it to become dark and self-destructive for others. For example, it's healthy to eat vegetables, but it isn't healthy to eat nothing but cauliflower every meal; exercise is a good self-care activity for anyone, but to relentlessly work out eight hours a day becomes self-punishment.

Applying the seven principles

How do we know when a self-care activity qualifies for the White Magic category? Ask yourself, *Does this activity and how I do it meet the standards set by our seven self-care principles?* Let's revisit those principles; they're listed below, together with the question you might ask yourself. Refer back to chapter 1, if you wish.

1. Self-care is a daily, lifelong practice. *Do I treat my self-care as the core of my well-being?*

2. Self-care is self-love. *Is this activity loving?*

3. Self-care means taking personal responsibility. *With this activity, am I taking responsibility for my present needs?*

4. Self-care means noticing what matters to us. *Does this action demonstrate what matters to me now?*

5. Self-care requires attention and responsiveness. *With this action, am I tending to my current needs? Am I willing to modify it based on changing circumstances?*

6. Self-care must be realistic to be effective. *Does it pass the reality test— is it sustainable? Am I truly willing and able to do this?*

7. Self-care precedes self-fulfillment. *Do I see how this action lays the groundwork for achieving my higher goals or needs?*

We can't hold all our self-care activities to every one of these stringent standards—as we'll see with Gray Magic, sometimes self-care means just having fun or breaking the rules. But these principles can serve as a gold standard for our self-care choices—as long as we remember that any good thing, taken to an extreme, can turn bad. And that brings us to the next kind of magic.

Black Magic Self-Care

Black Magic is the opposite of White Magic—it's self-care that employs our powers for activities that might appear to be self-caring but that most of us know, even while we're engaging in them, are bad ideas. Here are just a few of the ways that people engage in destructive, dangerous activities in the name of self-care:

- substance abuse: binge drinking, drug use
- other compulsive behaviors: disordered eating, compulsive overwork, shopping, exercise, extreme sports, and other dangerous activities
- self-harm actions, such as cutting, burning, or head-banging
- serial destructive relationships
- compulsive or addictive sex; obsessive use of pornography
- addictive gambling; compulsive or addictive gaming or Internet use

You may be wondering, *How on earth could those habits be classified as self-care? Those are bad, harmful, and potentially life-ending choices.* I would totally agree.

All of them are self-destructive, and yet I contend that they all also represent an attempt at self-care.

Hold on to your hat—I know that may seem outrageous. Yet, again and again, I have seen that when people first engage in these activities, it's simply to make themselves *feel* better, to decrease stress and anxiety, to numb uncomfortable feelings in general, and to increase feelings of well-being. People say to themselves, "I don't want to feel bad. I want to feel good, and this behavior takes the edge off my pain (or anxiety, or sadness, or sense of being overwhelmed). Yes, I know it can be harmful in the long run, but it helps me right now. So I'll take the chance."

We all understand the need to feel better. It's how we go about *getting* to that place that defines what kind of self-care we're using. As we begin an addictive behavior, we may feel like we're in control and can choose to turn on the "good" feelings at will to escape our discomforts. But soon we start seeking the escape for its own sake, and often we need more of the behavior to achieve that same result. That's when the behavior becomes an addiction. We become addicted to the altered state, the numbness, or even the shame that comes with the behavior (yes, one can even get addicted to the negative feelings that come with addictive behaviors). At that point, we're no longer aware of what motivated us to make the dark attempt at self-care in the first place. We are just obsessed with the addictive behavior itself. Brain chemistry and environmental components are involved, but the common denominator is loss of control.

When in recovery from an addiction, it's important to notice how you originally used the behavior as Black Magic self-care to escape from uncomfortable feelings and—especially important—to discover what those feelings were and are today. In doing so, we are able to find other methods of Gray or White Magic self-care to deal effectively with those feelings: activities that will actually support our health, well-being, and recovery.

The Black Magic kinds of coping will never give us the self-care we really need. No one has ever, after engaging in these behaviors, felt healthier, happier, and more in control, or had their life more together as a result. You will never see a book titled *Become an Addict: The Fast and Easy Way to Perfect Happiness, Joyous Relationships, Glowing Health, Career Success, and Financial Abundance.* You haven't seen this book because no one has that story. Rather, the stories we hear are from people who started out with all those things—to some degree—and ended up losing it all through addiction to one of these quick, dirty methods of dark self-care.

These Black Magic strategies generally lead to more self-destructive habits and fewer true, ongoing self-care behaviors. In other words, if you're engaging in Black Magic self-care, you probably aren't doing much White Magic. It simply doesn't occur to you because when you're using Black Magic self-care, the resulting addictions blind you to the fact that your health is failing, your relationships are falling apart, your job is in danger, and your bank balance is dangerously low. These are serious warning signs that you are already depleted and in need of a whole lot of the objectively good kind of self-care.

If you are trying to care for yourself in these ineffective, harmful, and potentially deadly ways and you've lost control, it's time to get help in the form of an addiction treatment program, a Twelve Step or other mutual-help group, psychotherapy, or all of the above. Almost all programs that treat addictions emphasize self-care as an essential component of recovery: creating community, developing an exercise routine, eating well, and surrounding yourself with supportive people are all factors that can prevent relapse. Another trick is to remember HALT: hungry, angry, lonely, or tired. These are signals that our self-care needs attention. If we don't respond to those needs, we're much more likely to resort to Black Magic self-care methods.

Addictive behavior can begin as an attempt at self-care, but of course, it's no substitute for the true ongoing self-care we need. Jennifer Matesa, author of *The Recovering Body* and *Sex in Recovery*, shared part of her own story of addiction and recovery with me.

> I "needed" to chew my pills [Vicodin] because I had so much else to take care of before taking care of myself. "I don't have time to take care of myself"—so went my rationalization. I woke by 6 a.m. so I could wake my son by 7 a.m. to get him washed, dressed, fed, and to daycare by 8 a.m., so that I could work from 8:15 a.m. to 1 p.m., when I picked him up from daycare and read to him before his nap. While he napped, I worked. Then I woke him and fed him a snack, sang with him in the car while running errands, brought him home, and set him up with toys while I made two dinners (one my husband would eat, one my

son would eat). Then I did a little housework or yard work or paperwork before putting him to bed at 9 p.m. After which, usually by 10 p.m., I would collapse. And also feel terrible because I was taking too little care of my marriage. All this was assuming my son didn't, for example, get sick. My schedule was the more flexible one, so I'd drop everything and take care of him. And all this was before the temptations of, say, streaming Netflix.

To keep up this schedule, I "needed" to chew Vicodin once or twice a day: first at 6 a.m. so I could face the day by numbing out my real physical pain and turning down the volume of the war in my mind. Also I sometimes chewed half a tablet at 4:30 p.m. when my energy was flagging and my head was starting to pound. To fit meditation, exercise, or deliberate, healthful, slow eating into a day like this one, I would have had to rob at least an hour of time from billable work or from caring for my son. Or I would have had to wake at 5 a.m.

Actually, what I really needed to do, and what I have done since quitting painkillers, was change the attitude with which I did my entire life. (When I first quit drugs, I was told in no uncertain terms by a recovering Percocet and methadone addict that I ought to "drop the Superwoman act." I was so far from my right mind that I had no idea what she meant.) Buying a stupid candle would not have made it any more possible for me to "take care of myself."

Chewing Vicodin, like all addictive behavior, is self-abandonment. What allows me to return to myself? Not just more yoga, more running, more organic food, more work. It's the loving, gentle attention I pay toward myself and my life. To cultivate this, I've had to realize I may not be able to renounce all addictive behaviors—eating chocolate, drinking caffeine, watching a marathon of *Orange Is the New Black*. Instead I try to treat myself with love and compassion when the stress overtakes me and I fall back onto those strategies.

One of the best ways to cultivate compassion for myself is to help other people cultivate self-compassion. So I participate in a very strong community of people, all of whom are working toward more self-love.

• • •

So although we can all agree that Black Magic self-care is not, in the end, a good thing, let's also understand that anyone doing it probably started it for reasons that seemed to make some kind of self-care sense. If your Black Magic self-care has become an addiction, the goal is to cease and desist, seek treatment, and adopt some of the other kinds of self-care that are actually supportive and nurturing.

Gray Magic Self-Care: The Middle Ground Can Be a Slippery Slope

I am about to tell you some truths you probably haven't heard before, some truths that will never find their way onto a bumper sticker.

There are times when . . .

- Splurging on a 400-calorie, five-dollar Frappuccino can be self-care (no matter what Suze Orman or Dr. Oz says).
- Dropping $150 on a pair of shoes can be self-care.
- Skipping a Saturday morning workout for donuts with your family can be self-care.
- Blasting '80s music on your drive home, instead of *All Things Considered* or an audiobook, can be self-care.
- Eating leftover birthday cake or cold pizza for breakfast can be self-care.

The form of self-care that falls into what I call the Gray zone is tricky. You know that these are not the highest and best forms of self-care, that you could or "should" be doing better—and you certainly aren't going to publicly announce them: "I gave myself permission to eat a brownie for dinner." But there are times when allowing yourself this type of self-care is a kind, loving, and responsive act. Remember principle 5? *Self-care requires attention and responsiveness.* That means we consciously think about our needs in the larger context of our life, and adapt our self-care practices accordingly.

Here's another example. After my busiest workdays, I give myself the gift of not removing my makeup before bed. Of course it isn't good for my skin, but just knowing that I'm going to let myself collapse after work is a comfort and a kindness to me. On those days, I also allow myself my weekly dose of the *Real Housewives of Wherever* while I eat an imbalanced dinner of cottage cheese and pineapple. Yes, I know it would be better if I ate salmon and a kale salad and read some Rumi after a long run. But after an extra-hard day I need to not think, and yes, I'm sure that mindfulness meditation would be better for me than an hour of Candy Crush. But life is not all vegetables and good behavior. Sometimes what looks like laziness or neglect, and probably wouldn't qualify as White Magic self-care, can actually be a caring and loving option when seen in context.

Here are a few examples of Gray Magic self-care in various shades—real examples from people I talked with:

- "Words with Friends or strangers or anyone who will reply on sleepless nights at 1 a.m."
- "After a tough week, I sometimes escape with a marathon session of Madden NFL 2017 with my old college buddy."
- "A stiff drink." (Which is different from several stiff drinks on a regular basis!)
- "I have deliberately eaten two Ghirardelli chocolate bars in one sitting. I also recently ate cookies and my BF's daughter's super-sweet pavé, and I've put on two pounds in the past month, but in the immortal words of some wise, self-accepting woman whose name I can't quite remember, screw it."
- "I sit and cry in the shower. I'm sure it looks like I'm wallowing, and I usually start by wallowing, but the white noise of the shower usually brings me around and I feel better."
- "There have been times when the lawn needs mowing and the toilet needs fixing, and that's when I decide it's time to go fishing."
- "Pinterest! I get lost in all the delicious images when real life, especially the news, gets too harrowing, depressing, or monotonous. The pins help me remember there is always beauty, wisdom, and humor in the world."
- "Staying in pajamas on Saturday morning and playing with my cat."

Now that we've learned there are Gray Magic self-care behaviors that can benefit us, we have to learn how to use them so they are truly self-care and don't morph into self-indulgence or neglect. Here are some ways to mindfully use Gray Magic.

Treats in lieu of self-care: The good, the bad, and the ugly
Remember that healthy-nutrition diagram issued by the U.S. Department of Agriculture in the 1990s? It was shaped like a pyramid. At the base was all the healthy stuff—vegetables, whole grains, fruits—that was supposed to make up the bulk of what we ate. The sweets and fats were at the tippy top, showing the small percentage that this category was to represent in our diets. Well, those sweets and fats are like the Gray Magic of self-care: the treats (food and otherwise) that we allow ourselves occasionally. We can have some treats, but they can't be our dominant method of self-care, or we will suffer consequences.

Author Geneen Roth has written extensively on the subject of compulsive overeating. One way to approach healing ourselves of compulsive overeating, she says, is to give ourselves exactly what we want to eat. But to do that, we need to be aware of what we really and *truly* want, and then give it to ourselves in a mindful and conscious way that allows us to fully enjoy each bite of what we have chosen. Sometimes giving ourselves the cheesecake or the two-hour tour of Pinterest is exactly what we need. But sometimes it isn't: when we know the cheesecake is a substitute for a hug or the Pinterest tour is a stand-in for a boundary we need to set with another person. These treats, these fishy rewards we throw at ourselves to reinforce behavior or acknowledge a job well done, are fine, but we can't live on just cheesecake. If we tried, we would very soon pay a price.

Roth also says that when we start to develop a relationship with our hunger, very often we want *all* the things we've deprived ourselves of. So in the beginning we want cookies, brownies, all the forbidden foods. But, says Roth,

> If you actually listen to your what body (not your mind) wants, you'll discover that it doesn't want three weeks of hot fudge sundaes despite the panting and salivating that is evoked at their very mention. . . . The moment you tell yourself you can have it, the moment the taboo is removed, hot fudge sundaes become as ordinary as sardines.[5]

I find the same is true with self-care. In occasionally allowing myself some Gray Magic self-care, I notice what makes me want that type of care. And by being mindful of what makes me feel like I deserve such an exception to the rule, I notice the behavior that may need to be changed. That's a chance to upgrade my methods from Gray to White Magic.

Upgrading from Gray to White Magic self-care

Are you engaging in too much Gray Magic self-care? Are those Gray methods becoming more frequent and perhaps even eclipsing the White methods? That's a good clue that something is seriously out of balance; something needs to give. We've been trying to care for ourselves with fixes—temporary indulgences—that are masking our real needs.

The first step in correcting this is to examine our current lives to see why we are Graying out. The second is to explore how we can increase our White Magic self-care in ways that make the Gray Magic less necessary.

Mary's story is a great example. A tax attorney who places a high value on fitness, she told me about her training regimen:

> There was a point in my life where I was training for a marathon. I was exercising a *lot* and eating really healthy. I decided that I could reward myself with a bowl of ice cream once in a while because I was doing so much great work for my body.
>
> But "once in a while" became almost every night, and instead of using it as a treat or reward, I started to feel deprived if I didn't have it. I also started to notice sluggishness in my running on mornings after the ice cream, which was defeating my biggest goal! Looking back, I started the ice-cream habit because I was pushing myself a little harder than I should have, and it all totally backfired. If I had been easier on myself in my training and dieting, I wouldn't have felt the need for a nightly bowl of ice cream.

Smart self-analysis, right? Gray magic—in this case, ice cream—can seem hard to resist if we're "pushing ourselves a little harder than we should have." Remember principle 6: *Self-care must be realistic to be effective.* Mary thinks her marathon-training regimen might have been a bit too strict. With more realistic standards, maybe the ice cream would feel less compelling.

But how do we know what the right standard is for us? It takes care and self-knowledge, and maybe some experimentation, to figure it out. That's why self-care is both an art and a science. And some people are really clever at it, as we'll see next.

SNEAKING IT IN

Did you know that Jessica Seinfeld—Jerry's wife—is a cookbook author? Her premise in *Deceptively Delicious* is to sneak healthy fruits and vegetables into kids' foods without them knowing. While I never personally tried any of her recipes, I saw her on *The Oprah Winfrey Show* and was impressed with her subterfuge.

Around that same time, I had some complicated paperwork that I really didn't want to do. Feeling both antsiness and ennui, I was avoiding it that day, wanting to be "anywhere but here." I'd been sitting in bed, papers on my lap. I had managed to turn my snuggle zone into an unpleasant and back-tweaking workstation. Curtains drawn. No light. No pillows to lean on. That's when the sneak-in method of self-care came to me, and I've been using it ever since.

In this methodology, I see how much healthy but rewarding self-care I can sneak into an unpleasant task: those situations that make me want to throw a tantrum about the unpleasantness of being an adult, then treat myself with a cookie, a quick tour through my email, or even more active procrastination. Now, my strategy is to sneak in as much nutritive self-care as possible. I ask, "*How can I add beauty, comfort, and kindness to this activity?*" There in my bedroom, I realized that in my resentful state of mind, I'd decided to make my paperwork as physically unpleasant as possible, to spur me on to the more pleasant activities waiting for me. But that motivation and self-cruelty were not working.

In an uncharacteristic move, I decided to add some pleasure to the equation, just as Jessica Seinfeld might add some yams to her meatballs. I got dressed, brewed a cup of Earl Grey tea, and went outside to work from a lounge chair in my backyard, accompanied by my dog and the Ella Fitzgerald station on Pandora. The task no longer felt so horrible. By adding some comforting Light Gray self-care to the task, I had found a way to whistle while I worked, leaving behind my old masochistic reflex to "work first, enjoy later." We all have some unpleasant but unavoidable tasks. Can you think of ways to balance those activities or settings with healthy self-care touches to make them more palatable? Of course, there are situations with no room for that—after all, you can't bring a candle, a teapot, and a cat to your mammogram appointment. But maybe you can plan to have lunch with a friend afterward and celebrate this very White Magic act of self-care.

While a friend of mine was studying for her psychology license, her money was tight. She'd be the first to tell you that her finances did not let her hang out at four-star hotels. But as her high-stakes exam date neared, that's exactly what she did to keep herself both calm and motivated. She budgeted for a glass of iced tea at a gorgeous hotel where she could sit in the gardens with her statistics books. A handsome waiter brought her tea, and she basked in the beauty of the grounds while studying.

As ongoing self-care, she also committed to preparing beautiful, nourishing food every day. Her meal presentations were so artful that she started an Instagram account where she shared photographs of her creations with her followers.

She passed her exam and got her license. Reflecting later on that high-pressure period of her life, she said, "Necessity is the mother of self-care! If I didn't care for me in whatever way I could, my soul would be utterly lost. These ways of caring for myself have been soul-saving."

What self-care principles was my friend using here? Certainly principle 2, *Self-care is self-love*. She deemed herself worthy of lovely treatment every day, and added a special occasion to boot. But also 6, *Self-care must be realistic to be effective*. She budgeted for a glass of iced tea in the hotel garden, not a full weekend in the honeymoon suite. And 5, *Self-care requires attention and responsiveness*. During a stressful time, she crafted the particular techniques that would answer her need to stay both motivated and connected with others.

• • •

White Magic, and various shades of Gray—all can be part of your self-care repertoire. To use them wisely, the key is self-knowledge. Take this quiz to see how you're currently using self-care magic.

 Life is not all vegetables and good behavior.

SELF-QUIZ

White, Gray, and Black Magic Methods of Self-Care

1. What do you consider absolutely essential White Magic self-care practices? Which of those absolutes are you doing? Which are you not making time and space for? No judgment: just notice.

2. What are your Gray Magic methods of self-care? (Go on, admit it: again, no one is here to judge you. The more you're aware of these methods, the less likely you are to blindly abuse them.) Which do you use regularly? Which do you only use when you are tired, stressed, hurting, or vulnerable?

3. How do you know when you're doing too much Gray Magic self-care? What consequences do you experience from overindulging in them? Which methods might be warning you to make changes in your life?

4. What Black Magic self-care methods have you used or are you currently using?

5. What support are you getting to engage in Black Magic self-care practices? If you've sworn off any of these, what support do you have to prevent yourself from going back to them?

6. What kind of self-care choices do you make when you are hungry, angry, lonely, or tired (HALT)? What's an example?

7. When you look at your daily schedule, how could you add some self-care, kindness, and love into your activities in both large and small ways? Now imagine that someone who loves you is keeping that schedule. Would you suggest revising it?

8. How might you, like Jessica Seinfeld, sneak some nutritive self-care into a "gotta do it" situation?

9. Remember: the whole point of sneaky self-care is that it is nourishing and has no consequences that leave you feeling worse. Make sure you've met your basic needs first (food, water, sleep, a safe environment); then sneak in something extra. Use as many senses as possible when adding self-care to a task.

   • Sound: How might you add music or other pleasing sounds? Or do you need earplugs or noise-canceling headphones or a white noise machine?

   • Smell: Might a bouquet of flowers, a dab of perfume, or even a "stupid candle" add to your self-care?

   • Take a breath. Are you breathing deeply? Are you catching yourself holding your breath? Would some deep belly breaths or diaphragmatic breathing help?

   • Remove distractions, irritations, and any punishing sensations that are affecting the moment. Ask yourself, is there a way you are making this task even more unpleasant? Can you think of any modifications you can make to change that?

   • Is there something you need from people in your life? Do you need a hug, some words of encouragement, a text to remind you that you are loved?

   • Is there a way to add pleasure or joy or play to this activity? Perhaps changing the location or adding an unexpected element? The answer to this one may not be immediate—but stay open to it.

By completing this exercise, you now have some valuable information to use as you proceed to chapter 4. You're about to do a self-care assessment, laying the groundwork for finding the personal fulfillment that quality self-care can bring.

PART TWO

Self-Evaluation

This above all: to thine own self be true.

—William Shakespeare

You Are Here

IMAGINE YOU'RE AT A SHOPPING MALL and you want to find that frozen-yogurt place—the one with that delicious low-fat yogurt topped with slivered almonds and chocolate chips. But it's not in sight. And where *are* you, anyway? What you might do, if you have any map skills, is begin by finding one of those mall maps. Then you'll study the map and look for the red dot that signifies *You are here*. From that point, it's easy to take action to get the yogurt.

Now consider where are you with your self-care. Where are you on the self-care map? That's what this chapter is all about. Let's start by getting a fix on where you are right now. In later chapters, you'll decide where you want to go with your self-care and how you might get there. The destination and the route you take to get there is entirely up to you!

Assessing Your Current Self-Care

As you begin this assessment, remember that no one else can see your answers. You'll benefit from this exercise only if you do it with brutal honesty.

Read through the areas of life listed below and think about how well are you doing on self-care. Rate yourself from 1 to 10, where 1 means *I have major room for growth in this area (and in fact I may not be doing anything)* and 10 means *I am the platonic ideal of perfect self-care in this area (and in fact I have a merit badge)*. I recommend you start with a blank page (on paper or screen) divided into three columns. In the left-hand column, list each of the twelve areas shown below and your numerical assessment of your self-care in that area. Give yourself plenty of vertical space between items.

___ my mental/intellectual life

___ my emotional life

___ my general care of my body

___ my close relationships (intimate, family, friends)

___ my everyday relationships (co-workers, acquaintances, customer-provider relationships)

___ my home environment (furniture, appliances, décor, and so on)

___ my possessions (technology, clothing, other objects)

___ my finances

___ my general time management self-care

___ my self-care in my work life

___ my leisure-time self-care

___ my spiritual self-care

Now scan your list and notice the range. Don't feel bad if in some categories you aren't doing diddly, or you have a whole lot of 1s and 2s. This truly isn't about judging yourself. Wherever you are is fine, you are fine, this is all going to be fine. Take a deep breath and see this as what it is: an opportunity for gathering information.

Are you surprised by the areas that might need some serious attention? Just notice that. Did you imagine you were more balanced in your self-care than you actually are? Or, conversely, are you pleasantly surprised by the results of this assessment? Whatever the case, just noticing what you are or aren't doing is the place to start. Give yourself credit where credit is due—it's okay to brag in your journal or to family and friends about it. Spell out where you really get this self-care thing, where you're knocking the ball out of the park.

Then look at the other areas. Given the challenges of living in today's complex world, there are probably some areas for improvement—but that's what this book is about. We'll figure out how you can move the needle up on these areas. So if some of your scores aren't as high as you'd hoped, fear not. We'll get you there. We'll discuss each of those topics in part 3 of this book.

What are you doing instead of self-care?

Take a look at those low-score areas and ask yourself, *What am I doing* instead *of self-care in this part of my life?* Reflect on the "non-self-care" habits we discussed earlier (listed below), and assign the best-fitting one to that area. Write it down in column 2.

- self-neglect
- self-sabotage
- self-betrayal
- self-sacrifice
- self-deprivation
- self-hatred
- self-harm

So let's say someone's list reads, in part, this way:

LIFE AREA RATING	NON-SELF-CARE BEHAVIOR	WHAT'S BEHIND IT
My finances: 2	self-neglect	
My time management: 6		
My work life: 3	self-sabotage	
My leisure time: 8		

What's standing in your way?

Now let's dig a bit deeper. For each of your low-score pairings, ask yourself what's behind your non-self-care in that area. What belief or concern keeps you from caring for yourself? Some common ones are listed here. Consider which ones might apply to you. Add your own as needed.

- ☐ It would be selfish of me.
- ☐ I don't have time for it.

☐ I don't have money for it.

☐ I don't think it would really make a difference in my life.

☐ I don't want to be alone with my thoughts, asking myself what I really need.

☐ I don't matter enough to do any self-care.

☐ When I do self-care, I feel guilty, like I don't deserve it.

☐ I'd rather have someone else take care of me in that area.

☐ Actually, I'm just fine without doing any self-care.

Now that list might look like this.

LIFE AREA RATING	NON-SELF-CARE BEHAVIOR	WHAT'S BEHIND IT
My finances: 2	self-neglect	I'd rather have someone else take care of me in that area.
My time management: 6		
My work life: 3	self-sabotage	I don't matter enough to do any self-care.
My leisure time: 8		

Your self-care self-analysis

Now comes the juicy part. For each of your low-score areas, write a paragraph (or a page or ten, if you are so moved) on *why* you're making those choices. Where did you learn these patterns of behavior? How exactly did they serve you, and how are they serving you now? To get started, consider the following prompts about your family of origin:

- How did your family members do self-care?

- How were you treated as a child?

- What messages did you get from your family members' habits of self-care (or non-self-care)?

- What impact have those messages had on your own self-care?
- What other internal and external messages stop you from caring for yourself?
- When you think about being good to yourself, is there a voice in your head that challenges you? What does it say that stops you?
- What about the voices you hear out in the real world?
- Are there people in your life now—or from the past—who stop you from taking better care of yourself?

This work can be very emotional. It may make you sad, upset, or angry—and that's okay. It can be hard to look at this stuff. It can be painful to see how our family members neglected themselves and how that affected us. And you might be surprised by the extent to which you are carrying around your family's beliefs. As hard as this can be to see, it will ultimately give you more freedom to make your own choices as an adult.

So, with an analysis, here's what a full financial self-care assessment might look like:

LIFE AREA RATING	NON-SELF-CARE BEHAVIOR	WHAT'S BEHIND IT
My finances: 2	self-neglect	I'd rather have someone else take care of me in that area.

Analysis: My parents never talked about money in front of the kids—ever. But they both worried about it, especially after their divorce. My mother once cried when I told her I needed new tennis shoes. She said she couldn't afford them—and that was the first time I knew that money was any kind of an issue for our family. So I learned that you don't talk about money, you don't think about it, and you certainly don't plan for what to do with it or celebrate what it can do for you. Even when her finances became more stable, my mother never spent money joyfully. There was always a grimness and a reluctance around money.

My response in my own life has been to be fearful of financial planning. That fear shows up in self-neglect: I just don't do it. I don't look at it. I leave it for my husband to take care of. I pretend that I don't have to bother or know. Part of me wishes that my parents had taught me how to take responsibility for my own financial well-being. That same part of me wishes they'd taken more responsibility for theirs. In the absence of that learning, I sort of blindly go "La-la-la-la-la" and hope someone else deals with it for me, as if I were still a little kid.

Good for you. You did some tough work there. Even if you only thought about these questions without writing them down, that may be more than you've ever done before. You can return to these self-assessment steps anytime to take a deeper look.

Your Self-Care Resources

Now that we've looked at your great and not-so-great areas of self-care, let's explore the resources you have to deal with those areas of weakness. Earlier we focused mostly on the "don't have" areas. This is the "do have" section. Hooray!

We've all probably had some experience with this kind of bad-news, good-news process. Maybe it was a job review where you knew in your heart of hearts that you were not the employee of the month. You saw your annual review, and instead of 9s and 10s there were 4s and 5s and phrases like "could use improvement," "not living up to your potential," "areas of needed growth include . . ." In a case like this, I hope the HR manager would take the time to list your strengths, too, so you'd feel motivated to improve and not sink into total despair.

I do the same in my work as a therapist. When I'm working with clients, we keep a running inventory of what kinds of resources they have to deal with the stressors they are facing, along with an inventory of the self-care areas that need a whole lot of work.

My method was inspired by my friend Monica, a busy mother in grad school. Her wise idea was a self-assessment of resources list based on the template of Maslow's hierarchy of needs. Remember that pyramid? At the bottom are our physiological needs; when these are met, we can start to meet our needs for safety and security, then for love and belonging, then for esteem and finally for self-actualization.

In this list, Monica followed that structure, starting with her physiological resources, and inventoried them all the way to the top.

MONICA'S INVENTORY OF RESOURCES

PHYSIOLOGICAL

☐ I can breathe, have good health, and sleep well at night.

☐ I have clean water to drink and good indoor plumbing.

☐ I have excellent food sources and enough money to buy the food.

☐ I have freedom of movement, with many places to exercise, both outdoors and indoors.

☐ Good clothing is available to me, and I have a washer and dryer to care for my clothes.

SAFETY

☐ I have a safe, warm home in a safe-enough neighborhood.

☐ Generally, the community is lawful and moral.

☐ Our household is supported by regular employment; our finances are stable enough that I can relax and expect consistency.

☐ We have health insurance and access to good medical care nearby.

☐ I have family, both nuclear and extended, with the security that offers.

☐ My home is clean and in decent repair with enough resources to maintain it.

☐ I have a car, the funds to keep it running well, and a good repair shop; I also have access to public transit.

LOVE AND BELONGING

☐ I have a husband who is supportive in practical ways as well as in helping me achieve my personal goals.

- [ ] I have children who love me.
- [ ] My parents live nearby and help out a great deal.
- [ ] I have in-laws almost as nearby who can help in emergencies.
- [ ] My best friend is of great emotional support.
- [ ] Women in a mother-daughter group I'm in are supportive, as are some mothers I know in my kids' school.
- [ ] I have options through the array of mental health professionals in my area.
- [ ] Our church offers activities and references to other help and resources.
- [ ] The college I attended is close by so I can tap into alumni services easily.

ESTEEM

- [ ] I am treated with respect.
- [ ] I feel I am capable of achieving things.
- [ ] I am reasonably confident.
- [ ] I do not directly experience race or gender discrimination.

SELF-ACTUALIZATION

- [ ] There are many excellent schools within a thirty-mile radius, both for children and higher education. Community colleges here are excellent, with resource centers and career guidance.
- [ ] As a student, I can get help at the career center or writing center, and talk with professors, librarians, or anyone else available on the support team.
- [ ] I can read, research, and learn, thanks to many resources: a good education, extensive library services, bookstores, local lectures, and a computer with Internet access.
- [ ] I belong to a strong faith community with many options available in our area.
- [ ] I have background as an artist; I also have personal freedom and art supplies so I can be creative in a variety of ways.

☐ I am personally very resourceful, so I tend to research any issue if there is a problem and find what I need.

Do you find that list as moving and inspiring as I do? If so, create your own resource list using Maslow's hierarchy of needs pyramid:

- physiological needs
- safety
- love and belonging
- esteem
- self-actualization

Keep in mind, this is not a list of what you feel you *should* have as resources or what you *wish* you had. Rather, it's an account of what you *actually* already have. And it might surprise you.

Here You Are

Now you have a really clear idea of where you are with self-care: you know which areas you're doing well in, which you're doing less well in, and what you're doing instead of self-care in those weaker areas. You've dug into the reasons you might be doing those things, and you've looked at what resources you have to address the major self-care needs in your life.

This is a fantastic place to be—and a place from which we can learn to get a whole lot better at self-care and reap its true rewards. That's what part 3 is all about.

 Cast aside the beliefs or concerns that keep you from caring for yourself.

PART THREE

The Magical Rewards of Self-Care

Love yourself first, and everything else falls in line.
You really have to love yourself to get anything done in this world.

—Lucille Ball

CHAPTER FIVE

Psychological and Emotional Self-Care

*The most powerful relationship you will ever have
is the relationship with yourself.*

—Steve Maraboli

IN THE ASSESSMENTS FROM CHAPTER 4, my bet is that most folks didn't have very many 10s in the areas of psychological self-care. It tends to get short shrift in a lot of people's self-care framework. One of the reasons for this, I think, is that people imagine psychological self-care to be something very formal or even exotic—like seeing a therapist or doing transcendental meditation. But if you listen to the psychological self-care suggestions from many experts in psychology, you'd actually hear a lot of basic, down-to-earth stuff involving the body and the senses.

What Works for You?

Even within the same profession, of course, people have varying needs: one person's healthy self-care work-life antidote is another's nightmare. Let's hear from three professional clinicians about their own self-care practices.

One psychologist friend explained what she does to take care of her psyche—and it didn't involve all the things I expected to hear from a woman with a passion for helping people. It's simply reading. "I can get lost in books," she told me. "Especially books on psychology and self-help give me a healthy kind of escape into a world of pure ideas. Many of these books offer a hope-in-a-bottle feeling . . . that all things are possible. Reading is also people-free and quiet. I need books and quiet and un-peopled time to do everything I need to do."

Notice that she's taken the time to figure out *why* her chosen activity is so important to her, what it gives her psychologically. The same goes for Ann and Lexa, a couple who can both talk with authority on Freud, dreams, and the unconscious. But they find their self-care refreshment in a totally different way, one that includes massages, golf, facials, and eating Fritos.

Ann puts it this way: "I am available to people all week, and being on the golf course is a time when it's okay for me not to be there for others. It reminds me that it is okay for me to have boundaries, to say no, and to not immediately respond to every text."

And the Fritos? That's Lexa. "I take really good care of myself all week—I exercise, I eat right, I do all the things I should do," she says. "A bag of Fritos reminds me that it isn't a zero-sum game, that I don't have to be perfect to be happy. And something as small as a bag of Fritos is a conscious reminder that I don't have to do this perfectly."

So for many people, psychological self-care involves a specific activity. For example, I've heard about sailing, which requires full but calm attention; drawing an illustration every day; vegetable gardening and cooking; and knitting, with its soothing, repetitive motion, to name just a few. Or it might involve nonactivity: simply sitting, taking an intentional break between tasks. Or it might be a quirky possession: "I have a goofy pink cell phone case," Jasmine confides. "It feels silly as a grown woman, but it really does make me smile whenever I see it, and these days we look at our cell phones a lot. It reminds me not to take life too seriously."

Find what works for you; then make a point of practicing it.

White Magic Psychological and Emotional Self-Care

Helping people take better care of their psyches is what I do for a living, so naturally I believe we can all work toward developing White Magic self-care habits in this area. But let me say for the record that, if asked, likely every therapist would have a set of suggestions somewhat different from mine, although we'd probably see some overlap, too. Like diets, sets of guidelines for mental and emotional health could reflect many different approaches. For the rest of this chapter, we'll explore the basics of White Magic psychological and emotional self-care as I see them. They include these guidelines:

- Monitor self-talk.
- Know and allow your feelings.
- Know your stressors.
- Have realistic expectations.
- Don't compare yourself to others.
- Forgive yourself.
- Let go of "pink cloud" positivity.
- Avoid the "never give up" myth.
- Promote genuine happiness.
- Live in the present with mindfulness.
- Stop lying to yourself.
- Know if you're an introvert or extrovert.

Monitor self-talk

Take some time to notice your self-talk. Would you talk to your child, lover, or best friend with that voice? If we had some kind of computer app that recorded our every thought, I think we'd be mortified to hear the many unkind ways we communicate to ourselves. Notice the tone and the negative judgments. Get to know the narrative of your internal bossy pants, inner critic, know-it-all, and Henny Penny "the sky is falling" worrywart. Taking the time to notice the way we torment ourselves with harsh criticism, unreasonable expectations, "shoulds," and general unkindness is one way we can start to make small changes. By challenging those messages and changing our self-talk, we can affirm our real assets.

Growing up in a family in the fashion business, with parents who prized appearances, I learned to greet myself in the mirror with an inventory of my faults—*Your figure's too this. Your eyebrows are too that. You need to change your hairstyle.* I'd contort and twist my face to better prove how crappy I looked, thereby upping my critical self-assessment.

At some point I decided that I needed to instead greet my reflection by looking straight into my eyes and saying warmly, "Hello, beautiful!" Yes, I know it sounds cheesy, like a Stuart Smalley line in *Saturday Night Live:* "I'm good enough, I'm smart enough, and doggone it, people like me!" But my fault-finding radar needed an interruption. At first I'd roll my eyes with disgust when I gave myself this incongruent greeting—I was faking it until I'd be feeling it—but in time it started to work. Today, that deep-seated inner critic still chimes in from time to time, but at the very least I'm starting the conversation by being kind and loving to myself. What's principle 2? *Self-care is self-love.*

With that one basic change, I came to identify all the things I say to myself that I would never say to another living soul. The simple act of recognizing our tone, as well as our words, when we speak to ourselves is an act of psychological self-care with big-time consequences. It can help us determine where we learned to talk to ourselves this way, and perhaps reveal some serious lack of self-love. Can you imagine greeting someone you love with a list of all their failings, then proceeding to chide and sneer at them? Productive, right? Change your self-talk, and you are on your way to doing better psychological self-care.

Know what you feel, then allow the feelings

This point may seem self-evident, but way too many of us are not okay with our feelings. Typically, only a few of our emotions make it into the "okay to feel" category. Our families of origin teach us which feelings are okay and which ones aren't. You likely won't be super surprised to hear that not all families are okay with anger or sadness. But there are others that aren't okay with joy or enthusiasm.

To take care of yourself psychologically, you need to identify what you are feeling *in the moment,* when you're feeling it. And that's harder than it sounds. Many of us, myself included, could often use some help in naming our feelings.

You may ask, "Why do I need to know how I feel?" It's a fair enough question. But here's the thing. Our emotions are a priceless signaling system. Among other things, they tell us what kind of self-care we need, where we might need to draw a line, what we love and what we don't. But if we're not listening, we can't learn from our feelings. (Principle 5: *Self-care requires attention and responsiveness.*) And by identifying the feelings that aren't so delightful— like grief, worry, hurt, annoyance, and envy, to name a few—we can begin to take them seriously.

Do you need help naming your feelings in any given moment? Let's say you're tired. Are you sleepy, lethargic, burnt out, listless, or depleted? The answer might help you decide what you need. To expand your vocabulary of feelings, use the list on the Center for Nonviolent Communication's website: www.cnvc.org/Training/feelings-inventory.

The simple act of naming feelings calms down the amygdala, or emotional response center of our brain. It's as if our brain is a fire alarm, and it keeps blaring the message to us until we finally pay attention and acknowledge the feeling. And experiencing the full range of our emotions (especially the unpleasant ones) is a necessary step in getting unstuck and finding authentic happiness and self-fulfillment. Painful feelings that aren't acknowledged or tended to are often repressed, resulting in depression, anxiety, and numbing of *all* of one's feelings. This increases the likelihood that we'll resort to the destructive methods of self-care we talked about earlier. I call this the "I had a bad day so I deserve a pony" method of self-care. Here's how it manifests: All of a sudden I'm feeling something unpleasant and I want to ignore it and feel something else, so I become that kid who wants a pony—only a pony will do. The "pony" can be a hot fudge sundae (or two), a glass of wine (or two), or something even more indulgent that will help me avoid my real feelings. While all those "ponies" are nice, none of them actually deal with the underlying crappy feelings that we believe make a pony necessary. The ponies distract us briefly with a new, different feeling, but they don't address the source of the pain. So, after that brief distraction, the icky feeling is back again and— surprise!—I need another pony.

At this point, I have a few options. I can (a) keep finding another pony; (b) find a whole herd of ponies; (c) withhold the pony and feel icky without figuring out why; or (d) determine what feeling I am trying to mask with the pony.

To practice White Magic self-care, the correct answer is (d).

Of course, there's some short-term discomfort when we go straight for the icky feeling—I hear you. But remember principle 3: *Self-care means taking personal responsibility.* Step up to the plate and choose option (d). If you don't identify the feeling, make space for it, and allow it to be there, you are soon going to have a whole fleet of ponies, a stable, and even a ranch as you keep upping the ante to feel better. And the further you'll be from experiencing the benefits of true, enduring self-care.

This amounts to abuse of Gray Magic self-care, where we try to explain away our feelings, a process I call "yes-butting" our feelings. "Yes, but . . ." is a technique I see a lot in therapy where people admit something that's harmful about their self-care—"Yes, it's true this isn't good for me . . ."—and then they add a "but" in which they justify their behavior and go back into denial: ". . . but I am super stressed out and tired, and don't have anything else to turn to." That's why we need to understand the motivation for our Gray Magic self-care, to ask what we're up to by seeking that new "pony." Is it a temporary indulgence, a quick fix to get us through a hard time until we get back on track with our ongoing White Magic self-care plan? Or has it become our *only* self-care plan, sliding into a pattern of Black Magic self-care to escape our real feelings? In the end, the more we try to "pony" away our pain, the greater the pain will eventually become and the more our unrecognized feelings build up.

Know your stressors: What are you worrying about?

A stressed person isn't necessarily an overworked, fried, type-A person who races around like a chicken with her head cut off. The truth is that we are all stressed. Stress, as defined by the pioneering endocrinologist Hans Selye, is "the non-specific response of the body to any demand for change."[6] Modern life bombards us with stressors, both good and bad: work, kids, relationships, family, traffic, long lines at the store, the nightly news, terrorism, climate change, and the voice-recognition software you have to joust with to pay your phone bill. Being conscious of what those stressors are makes it easier to adjust our self-care practices to deal with them. To take on a new stressor, you may have to expand your bandwidth, to use a digital analogy. And more bandwidth always comes with a cost. When you take on a new task, even a happy task, you have to pay the piper.

Imagine, for example, a newly engaged couple. They're happy—and yet there's a wedding to plan, family to deal with, perhaps a honeymoon in the works, maybe a move, finances to negotiate, and cake samples to taste . . . all without missing a beat in their normal responsibilities. Even in the best circumstances, it adds multiple stresses to their lives.

Many wonderful things can be stressors: winning the lottery, falling in love, buying a house, working toward a professional goal, training for a marathon, going on vacation. (I only hope you are having to up your self-care to deal with the stress of winning the lottery.) All stressors, good and bad, pull on our bandwidth. We might need to add a regular walk or run to work off the frazzle. Again, principle 5: *Self-care requires attention and responsiveness*. If we're aware of what stressors we are facing, we can adjust our self-care accordingly.

Have realistic expectations of yourself

One of the super gizmos I wish I had as a therapist is a magic expectation-shrinking device. Every day I hear people feeling guilty, sad, and generally awful because they've decided they should be more authentic, successful, peaceful, and mindful than they are, and a Zen master of compassion to boot. "I should be this. I should be that. I shouldn't feel this or that. I shouldn't care what people think." It's the "should" shuffle, and it's a lousy dance. Doing it generally results in standing still and feeling guilty, shameful, and just plain shitty.

So think of principle 6: *Self-care must be realistic to be effective*. Demanding perfection can really skew your priorities. You may not even know that your expectations are catawampus, so start listening for your "shoulds." Every time you start the "should" shuffle, ask yourself these questions:

1. How do I know this to be true?
2. Where did I learn this?
3. Is this rule applicable to everyone, or just to me?
4. Would I have this expectation of everyone I know?

5. Is this expectation making me feel good, happy, motivated? Or rather, is it making me feel stuck and sad?

6. Might there be a gentler, kinder, and less guilt- and shame-inducing expectation?

7. What is my fantasy of how life would be if I were living up to these "shoulds"?

Another super gizmo I'd like is the one that stops people from using text messaging to have emotional conversations and arguments, but I digress.

Stop comparing yourself to others

Or better yet, *accept yourself for who you are.* But that's a lot to ask all at once, so let's start with this: *stop comparing yourself to others.* And if you can't, at least understand what the heck you are doing when you engage in this activity.

Comparing yourself to others is an act of corrective psychological self-care related to the previous "should" shuffle. By comparing ourselves, we're trying—through an unhealthy and unkind method of self-care—to determine if we are okay, good, and lovable. And intrinsic in this action is a belief that our worthiness, happiness, and lovability depend on certain qualities that we may or may not possess. We are meaning-seeking creatures, always interpreting the stories, experiences, and images in our beautiful little brains. And all too often, we tell ourselves stories that take a narrow view of others' traits, perhaps to protect our own self-image. We may tell ourselves, "Mary got more attention because she was so pretty" or "My brother got more love and praise because he got better grades," "Fred is more appreciated than me because he's successful and makes lots of money," or "Kim has lots of friends because she has a nice house." We invent stories to make sense of our experiences, especially when they affect our sense of security and lovability. But too much of the time when we do this, as in the above examples, we pull out a measuring stick and come up with stories that suggest we *aren't* so good, smart, worthy, or lovable.

As soon as we pull out that measuring stick, we're engaging in a fallacy: we're interpreting another person's attributes (physical traits, grades, income, possessions, and so on) as a determinant of our own worth or happiness. For example, Sally has a fancy new car, and I've decided that my lovability and happiness are compromised because I can't afford one. But wait! There are millions of people *without* new cars who feel lovable and happy; Sally has likely experienced many periods of lovability and happiness in her life without owning a new car; there are millions of people with new cars who *don't* feel lovable or happy. I often hear from clients who have achieved some goal they longed for—like buying a new car—and now they feel sad and disappointed. The magic didn't happen. Some respond to this by deciding they really need some *other* trait, object, or experience to feel happiness. So then they're right back to where they started.

It may be a question of principle 4: *Self-care means noticing what matters to us.* What *really* matters, beyond the car or the salary or the Blahniks? Remember this: everyone, and I mean *everyone,* has doubts, fears, and insecurities. No one has it all together—no one—no matter how good they look, how great their story sounds, how picture-perfect their persona. No set of external circumstances can guarantee happiness.

This reality actually is a hard pill to swallow for many people. It is a strangely comforting (and yet simultaneously masochistic) fantasy to believe that there's some guaranteed path to happiness: 4.0 GPA, admission to Stanford, a job at Google, married by thirty, 2.0 perfect kids by thirty-five, the body fat of an Olympian, and a retirement portfolio that would impress Warren Buffet. We see other people achieving those things and tell ourselves that if we could just be like them—if only we were taller/shorter, funnier/stronger, more educated/more street-smart, you name it—we could have it all, which means a life devoid of hurt, sadness, and want.

No one has it all, and at the root of the comparison trap is the faulty logic that having a certain attribute will guarantee a certain outcome, and it simply isn't true.

If you were operating under this fallacy, please know that you're not alone. Many of us learned it from parents, our culture, TV and movies, social media, friends, bosses, and work associates. The world perpetuates a pernicious mythology that certain things guarantee happiness and success. And the world holds up successful people and celebrities as ideals to prove the point. Ironically enough, there are entire industries that report the breakups, bankruptcies, divorces, and dramas of all the people who seemingly have it all. That's

59

the bread and butter of the tabloids and talk shows. So why do we continue to believe there are happiness guarantees out there and that if only we could be like so-and-so, we too could cash in?

When you catch yourself comparing yourself to others, challenge yourself. Gently interrupt your thinking and bring in this self-care reminder instead: "By comparing myself to this person, I'm buying into the myth that certain circumstances can guarantee happiness. By using a measuring stick to compare us, I'm shortchanging both of us."

Yes, it's a mouthful, but no one said that self-care was easy.

Forgive yourself

Self-Care To-Do List

☐ Beat myself up for past wrongs with great regularity.

☐ List all my failings daily, spend an hour every morning reviewing every poor decision I ever made, and give myself hell for it.

Can you imagine a self-care list that starts with these tasks? Of course not. But you may be doing these very things. Regrets, recriminations, guilt, embarrassments, and wishing for a do-over can reinforce the delusion that "I am bad, unworthy, a failure, and there's nothing I can do about it." The truth is that you don't have a DeLorean time machine and you can't go back to the future. But one thing's for certain: spending too much of the present focusing on the past will end up being a regret in your future.

You may be thinking that if I knew of *your* horrible choices and mistakes, I would agree that they are unforgivable. I'm here to say that like everyone else alive, you have made mistakes, have done some things you wish you hadn't, and feel some guilt and shame about it. I'm also here to say that you can get over it.

As a therapist, I love it when clients get past their shame and finally admit out loud what they believe makes them a bad, unlovable human being. There is often a disclaimer before they confess: "You're going to think I'm a horrible person . . ." I can tell you that, without fail, what they did is never as bad as they think it is, and 99 percent of the time they have punished themselves for it more than I or anyone else would ever think of doing. Rather, my reaction is to feel empathy and even more compassion for them than I did before they so bravely made themselves vulnerable.

Don't get me wrong here: of course there are acts of cruelty and abuse that require amends and sometimes legal consequences. But for the most part, when people reveal their past wrongs and harms, they discover that making mistakes is a part of being a flawed human who deserves forgiveness. That's principle 3, *Self-care means taking personal responsibility*, tempered with principle 2, *Self-care is self-love*.

One of the gifts of therapy is to understand your behavior and become accountable for yourself. But that doesn't mean torturing yourself for the past; it means learning from your past, making amends to yourself and others, and then extending kindness, compassion, and mercy to yourself.

Try using this self-forgiveness process to help you move on.

Think back to something you regret, and fill in the blanks.

- ☐ The thing I can't stop beating myself up for is _____.
- ☐ Looking back with eyes of compassion, I understand that my choice to do this was motivated by _____ (for example, fear, lack of awareness, insecurity, scarcity).

Then ask yourself:

- ☐ If someone I loved made the same decision or took the same action, could I forgive them?
- ☐ If so, why are they more deserving of forgiveness than I am?
- ☐ If my loved one couldn't forgive themselves, what would I say to them?

Finally, ask yourself:

- ☐ What do I gain by not forgiving myself?
- ☐ How might I be denying my power in the present by holding on to the past?
- ☐ What can I learn from this situation? How can I use it to make better choices now?
- ☐ What might I be grateful for in this situation?

Let go of "pink cloud" positivity

I know that thinking positive is considered an absolute self-help tenet. But I am daring to differ with this undisputed truth. You see, I believe that positivity can be, in some cases, a way to engage in a hopeful delusion—called "pink cloud" thinking in recovery circles—that doesn't require us to show up, take action, and do the real down-and-dirty legwork that is actually necessary to take real care of ourselves. To just blithely believe everything will work out for the best without taking wise action is to abandon oneself. A good attitude is great; action paired with a good attitude is even better.

I'm not asking you to be Debbie Downer and surrender to pessimism (that, too, is predicting outcome without evidence). Instead, the most self-caring stance you can take is looking at the reality of your life, facing it, and not going into extreme pessimism ("There is nothing I can do") or into extreme positivity ("I need do nothing because everything will be okay if I am just positive").

Positivity doesn't keep you healthy if you are living on a diet of doughnuts, denial, and destructive behavior. (An Arab proverb says, "Trust God, but tie your camel down," meaning yes, have faith, but don't be an idiot. Scholars may disagree on my nuanced interpretation, but that's the core of it.) Yes, fine, go ahead and expect the best, see your glass as full or empty, or don't have a glass at all. But ground your actions and expectations in reality. Principle 6: *Self-care must be realistic to be effective.*

Avoid the "never give up" myth

If you read my previous book, *The Next Happy,* you know that I am a recovering "never-give-upper," and I know I'm not alone in this. Our culture believes so strongly in that myth that a whole lot of us just don't know when, or if, it is ever okay to walk away from something. We are so afraid of being quitters, losers, and failures that even when the pursuit of keeping a dream alive is making us sick, we believe we have to obey what Winston Churchill said: "Never, ever, ever, ever, ever give up."

Churchill gave that particular speech about keeping the Nazis from entering Britain, and in that endeavor, the quote fit. But there are times when the sanest, most self-loving option is to stop doing something. Ask yourself: *Is the pursuit of this goal, dream, or hope improving my life? Or am I living my life on layaway, delaying all my happiness for some glorious day when this will be all worth it?* Even if your dreams aren't at the destructive level, it's an enormous act of self-care just to make space in your mind to consider that sometimes letting go and moving on is the right, good, and healthy choice. "Never give up" is rigid, harsh, and makes no exceptions—and that is antithetical to real self-care.

We might even invoke principle 7: *Self-care precedes self-fulfillment.* When our fixation on a goal has superseded our quality of life and our self-care, let's reevaluate. Even if we were to finally reach that goal, how fulfilling would it be if we've lost our self in the process?

Promote genuine happiness

Self-care is to a large extent a framework for seeking happiness. But too often, we think of happiness not as deep satisfaction but as a perpetual high. Some of the reasons people turn to Black Magic self-care is that they want to get to those high, happy feelings super fast. And quick fixes like drugs, alcohol, and sex can instantly change our mood from sad to serene, depressed to delighted, angry to amiable.

In his book *Stumbling on Happiness,* psychology professor Daniel Gilbert shows that what we tend to think will make us happy (more money, more stuff, just more in general) isn't what really makes us happy.[7] Recall principle 4: *Self-care means noticing what matters to us*—what *truly* matters.

According to author and researcher Sonja Lyubomirsky, half of our capacity for happiness is genetically determined, 10 percent is situational, and 40 percent of it is up to us.[8] Her studies show some of the big factors for creating happiness—and they aren't about more stuff or more money. Here's what she recommends:

- *Have quality relationships.* Maintain social circles with people you care about and who care about you. You don't need lots of relationships to be happy; you need *quality* relationships.
- *Don't hold grudges.* Lyubomirsky claims that having enemies is deleterious to our happiness. Everett Worthington and Michael McCullough's research demonstrated that forgiving others results in more positive emotions for us.[9]

- *Be grateful.* Gratitude is "a kind of meta-strategy for achieving happiness," says Lyubomirsky. "Expressing gratefulness during personal adversity like loss or chronic illness, as hard as that might be, can help you adjust, move on, and perhaps begin anew." So how to practice gratitude? Writing gratitude letters and gratitude journals are both wonderful ways. I recommend digging for details: *I'm grateful for my house,* yes, but spell out what you love and appreciate about it, how its rooms make you feel. When you recognize these specifics, you are more likely to really feel the gratitude.

- *Give to others; practice generosity.* We all sort of know this works, and yet very often we try to acquire and achieve our way to happiness. Ebenezer Scrooge is a prime example. It took a run-in with three ghosts and a preview of his gravesite to wake him up, but he did, eventually, learn his lesson and presumably spent the rest of his life practicing generosity. Random acts of kindness and generosity make people happier. And according to Lyubomirsky, *these acts need not be random, or anonymous, or any kind in particular:* "We have found that almost any type of acts of kindness boost happiness." They also boost social connectedness, inspiring "pay it forward" impulses that multiply the effects.

- *Take good care of your body.* We will talk a lot more about this topic in the next chapter on self-care and your body. For now, all you need to know is that there is a lot of evidence that a habit as simple as getting twenty minutes a day of aerobic exercise can enhance your mood and decrease depression, thereby upping your happiness.

Be mindful: Live in the present.

How do we learn mindfulness? Research has shown the benefits of meditation practices, and there are many other resources for developing the skill of being in the present moment.[10] But you don't need to be a meditator or a follower of Zen to be mindful. Should meditation not be your thing (and it most certainly isn't mine), there are other mindfulness practices that get us out of the past, the future, and the constant mental multitasking that keeps us stressed, distracted, and overwhelmed. And the benefits of mindfulness spill into many areas of our lives.[11]

Anything that gets you into the now can work, including following the Twelve Step maxim "One day a time" or spiritual teacher Ram Dass's advice, "Be here now." I have a practice of "thought-stopping" where I first notice that I am in the past or future, and then give myself the option of returning to the now. Practicing mindfulness can be as informal as taking a series of belly breaths that bring you into the now, or as formal as a two-hour-a-day meditation practice. Either way fits fine with principle 1: *Self-care is a daily, lifelong practice.*

It isn't easy to break our habits of busyness, of being anywhere but here, so it can be very helpful to find a class, adopt a meditation practice, or develop your own tools for learning to live in the present.

Recognize your distorted thinking

All of us are prone to habitual thoughts that don't reflect reality: *cognitive distortions,* in the words of Aaron Beck, the founder of cognitive-behavioral therapy. These distortions are often negative, wrong, irrational, held as fact, and habitual. They color the way we see the world, and it is possible to go through your entire life without recognizing or challenging them.

The process of identifying what cognitive distortions you are prone to, catching them, and changing them is serious psychological self-care that will benefit your self-concept, relationships, and general emotional state in substantial ways. People with greater cognitive distortions are more likely to struggle with depression, anxiety, and higher levels of stress.

David Burns, the author of *Feeling Good: The New Mood Therapy,* listed some of the common cognitive distortions that can truly mar our view of ourselves and the world.[12]

1. *All-or-nothing thinking:* Thinking of things in absolute terms, like "always," "every," or "never." Few aspects of human behavior are so absolute.

2. *Overgeneralization:* Taking isolated cases and using them to make wide generalizations.

3. *Mental filter:* Focusing exclusively on certain, usually negative or upsetting, aspects of something about yourself while ignoring the rest, like a tiny imperfection in a piece of clothing.

4. *Disqualifying the positive:* Continually "shooting down" positive experiences for arbitrary, ad hoc reasons.

5. *Jumping to conclusions:* Assuming something negative where there is no evidence to support it. Two specific subtypes are also identified:
    a. Mind reading: Assuming the intentions of others.
    b. Fortune telling: Predicting how things will turn out before they happen.

6. *Magnification* and *minimization:* Inappropriately understating or exaggerating the way people or situations truly are. Often the positive characteristics of *other people* are exaggerated and negative characteristics are understated. There is one subtype of magnification—*catastrophizing:* focusing on the worst possible outcome, however unlikely, or thinking that a situation is unbearable or impossible when it is really just uncomfortable.

7. *Emotional reasoning:* Making decisions and arguments based only on how you *feel* rather than also taking objective reality into account.

8. *Making "should" statements:* Concentrating on what you think "should" or "ought" to be rather than the actual situation you are faced with, or having rigid rules that you think should always apply no matter what the circumstances are.

9. *Labeling:* Explaining behaviors or events merely by naming them; related to overgeneralization. Rather than describing the specific behavior, you assign a label to someone or yourself that puts them in absolute and unalterable terms.

10. *Personalization (or attribution):* Assuming you or others directly caused things when that may not have been the case. When applied to others, blame is an example.

Since I am a therapist, it may not surprise you that I suggest therapy to reap the full benefits of this or any other method of recognizing the lies you may be telling yourself—especially if you find it hard to recognize and challenge them on your own. A qualified therapist can also help you identify the behavior patterns that may result from these distortions. These benefits can truly be life changing. Uncovering your distorted thinking takes courage and commitment, but remember principle 3: *Self-care means taking personal responsibility.* Taking charge of your own thoughts is high-level accountability. Welcome to that challenge.

Know if you're an introvert or an extrovert

This knowledge can have a surprisingly large impact on your self-care choices. Are you an innie (introvert) or outie (extrovert)? You may know your type from the Myers-Briggs temperament sorter or another source. But first, let's go back to the father of this concept, psychologist Carl G. Jung. In his book *Memories, Dreams, Reflections,* Jung defined these two "attitude types": introverts are oriented in life "through subjective psychic contents" (focusing on one's inner world); extroverts have a "concentration of interest on the external object" (the outside world).[13] In practical terms, this means that extroverts gain energy by being around other people and feel drained if they spend too much alone, while introverts thrive on that alone time. So, we tend to recharge our brains either in an introverted way or an extroverted way. This doesn't mean that extroverts can't be alone or that introverts can't be with people.

Susan Cain, author of *Quiet: The Power of Introverts in a World That Can't Stop Talking,* explains that introverts "may have strong social skills and enjoy parties and business meetings, but after a while wish they were home in their pajamas. They prefer to devote their social energies to close friends, colleagues, and family. They listen more than they talk, think before they speak, and often feel as if they express themselves better in writing than in conversation. They tend to dislike conflict. Many have a horror of small talk, but enjoy deep discussions."[14]

Once you know which you are, it is part of your psychological self-care to notice if your introversion or extroversion needs, the sources of your psychological fuel, are being adequately met. I am a very strong introvert—from an extroverted family—who has a job and a life that is full of people. This is fine, because my work is with people I develop a deep connection with, which

I find invigorating. But after a day of doing that work, making small talk at a cocktail party would be unthinkable for me. My introversion requires that I have time when I am alone with my thoughts in a quiet and empty space. All this time alone looks to my extroverted partner like something akin to punishment. After his day at work, he wants to go out, see people, do stuff. Part of my self-care is sometimes saying that I need to recharge and that I simply can't go out with him. Sunday nights for me are a stay-at-home time when I don't go out to dinner and socialize; it is some of my most important and nonnegotiable self-care.

In a society that is primarily extroverted in its focus, we introverts often feel sheepish about our need for nonpeopled quiet. Even as a therapist, and as a self-described introvert since childhood, I had a major aha moment in a dream when I heard the following words: "Introversion is not pathology." I awoke feeling liberated from my contortions to be an extrovert. Later, Susan Cain's book gave me full permission to modify my life and notice what suited me best. Knowing and responding to your introversion or extroversion will likely mean modifying your self-care based on what feeds you uniquely.

•   •   •

We've spent a lot of time in this chapter inside our heads, so it's time now to get physical. In the next chapter we'll explore what fully conscious self-care means in relation to our bodies.

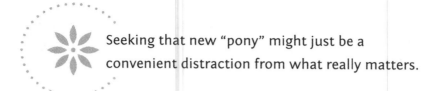

Seeking that new "pony" might just be a convenient distraction from what really matters.

SELF-QUIZ

Your Psychological and Emotional Self-Care

1. What psychological self-care are you doing? What specifically works for you?

2. What White Magic self-care do you do?

3. What kind of self-talk are you giving yourself? Would you talk to others the way you talk to yourself?

4. Are your feelings allowed? Which ones? What feelings are most definitely not allowed? How do you make space for your feelings?

5. How do you engage in Gray or even Black Magic self-care as a way to deal with feelings that you aren't okay with?

6. What stressors are you facing now, and how might those stressors affect the kind of self-care you need now?

7. What kind of expectations do you have of yourself? Are your expectations loving and caring, or more cruel and unrealistic?

8. Are you comparing yourself to others? And if so, how have you been doing that in the guise of taking care of yourself?

9. What do you need to forgive yourself for? Are you holding on to unforgiveness in a way that is hurting yourself?

10. Are you using positive thinking in a way that is hurting you? Might it be more self-caring to allow yourself some more nuanced thinking?

11. Are you pursuing a goal or dream in a way that is hurting you? Are you living your life on layaway, delaying happiness for some glorious day when "this will all be worth it"?

12. What are you doing to promote your genuine happiness?

13. How are you or aren't you promoting mindfulness in your life?

14. What distorted thinking are you engaging in that is self-harmful?

15. Are you an introvert or an extrovert? How do you need to take your temperament into account in your self-care plan?

CHAPTER SIX

Self-Care and Your Body

Do something every day that is loving toward your body and gives you the opportunity to enjoy the sensations of your body.

—Golda Poretsky

YES, THIS CHAPTER IS ABOUT YOUR PHYSICAL BODY: how you're taking care of it and maybe how you could do a better job. But I promise, I will not bossy-pants tell you what to do and how to do it. I will most certainly not advise you how to eat and exercise, how much water to drink, or how to decrease inflammation seventeen ways; all that goes into the category of White Magic self-care that you will determine for yourself. I'm not going to impart a lot of *Thou shalts* and *Thou shalt nots* to live by, especially in regard to eating low-carb, Paleo, wheat-free, meatless, or whatnot.

And to be honest, I simply don't believe—and I know this is heresy—that there is any one way of taking care of your beautiful, unique, idiosyncratic, and ever-changing body. Different strokes for different folks. Now, I understand that some people's self-care includes strict adherence to a certain way of eating and exercising that they believe is the only way to live a healthy life. And that's fine, too, as long as they let me eat my carbs in peace. (Hold the gluten lecture, please.)

I'm not here to develop a White Magic self-care plan with you, but I do want to help you be more conscious of your patterns. As you read this chapter, keep these questions in mind:

- What are you doing (or not) for physical self-care? Why or why not?
- How might you be using your self-care rules in ways that help you—and ways that hurt you?
- What Gray Magic self-care are you doing that might be a *higher* level of care than you think?
- What areas of physical self-care might you be shirking on?
- How might you do a better job by making some philosophical switcheroos that could be more caring?

First, let's review the shades of self-care as they might apply to our bodies.

White Magic: This is the stuff you believe absolutely must happen for your optimal physical health. These are the self-care activities you truly believe in; for example, "I will eat this and I won't eat that. I will see my doctor every year for a physical. I will floss my teeth. I will exercise at least twenty minutes daily." They're the goals you have for yourself, even if you aren't always acting on them.

Gray Magic: These are the temporary, situational self-care remedies you may be turning to when you aren't getting enough rest, food, water, touch, sleep, movement, stress relief, or medical attention. These "quick fixes" have their place, but they may be a clue that you need to up your self-care game, especially if they become habitual and begin to replace your White Magic self-care activities. A Frappuccino does not make up for lack of sleep. A massage does not compensate for the fact that you've been hunched over a computer for ten hours a day.

Black Magic: These are self-defeating methods of self-care often used to "self-medicate" emotional or physical discomfort. They include alcohol and other drug abuse, compulsive sex or gambling, and masochistic behaviors. They are clearly *not* good ways to care for your precious body, yet they may be misguided attempts to ease pain, stress, and fatigue. In the end, they offer only the illusion of feeling better and will cause harm to your body, mind, and spirit. These behaviors often lead to addiction, resulting in loss of control and even death. Once people are in the danger zone of using these methods, they require professional help and ongoing recovery support.

Your Body and Your Self-Parenting Style

In your self-assessment in chapter 4, you may have analyzed how your parents modeled self-care for you and how that might still affect you today. We often take on the role of our parents in creating a *self*-parenting style that can influence how well or poorly we care for ourselves. When it comes to physical self-care, the style we use has major consequences.

The indulgent style: Neglect in disguise

For example, there's the permissive or indulgent self-parenting style: the "I can have whatever I want with no limits" approach to self-care that lets you skip over any of the less pleasant tasks of having a body, including physical exams, routine tests, flossing, dental visits, accepting that you need eight hours of sleep, and other basic maintenance requirements. These tasks are like the oil changes and tire rotations your car needs to keep running well over the long term. And ignoring them really is a form of neglect that can have a whole lot of serious and life-threatening consequences, including heart disease, stroke, diabetes, cavities, gum disease . . . you get the picture. Giving yourself everything you want, choosing to do only what feels good and tastes good, and ignoring the ordinary but necessary care and maintenance of your physical self is not only poor self-parenting; it's self-destructive.

If this is you, think about your own family of origin. Maybe your parents modeled the indulgent style for you, or maybe they did the opposite—in which case you might still be trying to overcompensate for their authoritarian style. Let's take a closer look at that.

The authoritarian style: A big fat setup

Every year on New Year's Eve, people list their White Magic self-care plans: "This year I won't eat sugar." "I will exercise three hours a day, seven days a week." "I'm going vegan, and I will lose twenty pounds by Valentine's Day." But even before the confetti is swept up and the champagne glasses are put away, thousands of people have already given up on their authoritarian self-care programs. Why? Because the first time they eat a cookie, miss a work-out, or crave a hamburger, they decide they can't live up to that demanding regimen. (Remember principle 6: *Self-care must be realistic to be effective.*)

73

Unfortunately, a lot of folks tell themselves, "If I can't do this perfectly, there's no point," and they give up, full stop. Or they become the rebellious child and say to themselves, in effect, "Get off my back. You can't tell me what to do!" Or they tell themselves, "I screwed up today, but I'll get back to it; I'll start again tomorrow" (or next week or next month), when in fact, no waiting is necessary to restart the program, perhaps on a more realistic basis. The authoritarian approach to self-care is an illogical and ill-conceived strategy that rarely leads to what you set out to achieve, let alone happiness. In fact, it's a big fat setup. And I know a whole lot about it from personal experience. For many years, I had an eating disorder that was all about perfection and all-or-nothing thinking. A true cognitive distortion, right? It resulted in self-loathing because I couldn't live up to my own unreasonable, unhealthy rules for eating. Now, most of us don't put things like "Don't eat today" at the top of our to-do list, like I did. But we may set ourselves up in other ways. And then, with the slightest deviation from the ideal, we backlash, giving ourselves total permission to take the indulgent extreme.

Here is an example of how such decisions are made: "I'm so lazy; I promised myself I'd run this morning and I wouldn't have a muffin with my coffee at Starbucks, but I blew it on both counts. Okay, fine! Since I clearly don't have the discipline, I might as well just eat whatever I want today." Sound familiar? If so, let me introduce you to something called the middle ground.

Finding a middle ground

People who engage in a lot of White Magic self-care from an authoritarian perspective tend toward all-or-nothing thinking. They have to work a little harder to see the benefits of the middle ground. But they do learn, and soon they're saying things like, "I'd like to work out every day, but I can't—so I'll take a walk on my lunch hours and take a Sunday exercise class at the Y."

That goes for me, too. As a person with some perfectionism and a history of disordered eating and exercising, I've always had pretty high White Magic self-care expectations in this arena, and I finally learned to scale them back. Still, I don't always deliver: I'd give myself a B overall, rather than an A.

For example, I believe I should drink eight glasses of water a day, but I don't. There are days when I drink no water. I believe I should eat four daily servings of vegetables and three of fruit, but yesterday that amounted to a few bites of coleslaw and some grapes in the form of a glass of red wine. I believe I should be doing thirty minutes of cardio daily and weights three times a week. But this week, I've done only two exercise videos. Because I am not living up to my White Magic ideals, I give myself a B.

For me, that is adequate. As a therapist, I feel more strongly about earning an A in mental and emotional self-care—and I do earn that A. For me, scaling back my perfectionism in physical self-care is a victory. And this is a common problem. Jill, a client of mine, struggled with an all-or-nothing approach to diet and exercise, too. Her regimen for both was strict, and if she broke with it, she'd attack herself for not living totally in the White zone. I introduced an idea: could she sneak in a little White Magic self-care after she'd broken one of her rules? After eating a forbidden breakfast burrito, for example, she could give herself something she felt was good for her—perhaps take her multivitamin, have a shot of wheat grass juice, or eat a carrot. That might help her avoid kicking herself and abandoning her plan for the rest of the day. At first she balked at this method, not believing it would do any good, but she began to do it nonetheless. When she missed her 5 a.m. yoga class, she did some gentle stretching for five minutes—a tiny bit of good self-care that took her out of the all-or-nothing mentality. Soon she found herself leaving behind her authoritarian model of self-care. She found that she preferred to eat foods that supported her health and gave her energy for daily yoga, stretching, or walking. She reports, "I mostly take care of me in a better way now, and some days I have a cookie, and it doesn't define me. It isn't a failure—it's just a cookie."

For Jill, finding the middle ground meant switching from a no-sugar to a low-sugar diet. "Before, I failed so often on no-sugar plans, and I always beat myself up," she told me. "But now if I have some sugar, it isn't the end of the world, and it isn't an excuse to eat every cookie in the house with the promise that 'this is the last time ever.' After eating something on my naughty list, I immediately do something good and kind for my body instead of punishing it. I've lowered my sugar intake a lot and I've noticed a *huge* difference in how I feel after I eat it now. Except I do love dark chocolate! But now, when I eat it, it's no longer a failure or an excuse to self-destruct."

So we all prioritize our areas of self-care and the habits we cultivate in each area. Here's an example: my own top 20 habits for physical health and well-being.

TRACEY'S TOP 20 PHYSICAL SELF-CARE HABITS

1. I sleep at least eight hours a night, on a high-quality mattress. I schedule my work so I can get adequate rest. Plenty of sleep is a nonnegotiable for me.

2. I eat wholesome and nutritious foods, with an occasional super-high-quality salted oatmeal chocolate chip cookie and gnocchi with pesto sauce.

3. I unapologetically enjoy an espresso with half-and-half and sugar every morning.

4. I drink a glass of red wine every night; sometimes two, but never more than that.

5. I take supplements every day: a multivitamin, a B-complex, vitamin D, calcium, and omega-3 fatty acids.

6. I've hired a trainer to come a couple of times a week to help me get on a self-care exercise plan.

7. I wear a seatbelt.

8. I take very good care of my skin: I apply sunscreen, hand cream, and lip balm daily.

9. I have my hair done by a competent stylist, I deep-condition my hair weekly, and I have my eyebrows tinted.

10. I get biweekly manicures and pedicures.

11. I refuse to wear anything that inflicts pain: shoes that pinch, bras with stabbing underwires, scratchy sweaters, too-snug pants.

12. I always bring a sweater or a jacket with me when I go out, as I easily get cold.

13. I consistently maintain my weight.

14. I roll on a foam roller to ease the hip and back pain that comes from sitting long hours at work. Whenever I have pain, I seek to understand the source of it and how I can relieve it.

15. I have trustworthy doctors with whom I can be honest and who will listen to me.

16. I see my doctor every three months to manage my thyroid condition; I have a yearly Pap smear and mammogram.

17. I wear perfume that makes me happy.

18. I cuddle with my dog as one form of comforting touch.

19. I take baths using Epsom salts, lavender oil, and baking soda.

20. As an evening enhancement, I light a Diptyque Feu de Bois candle, reminding myself that I can rest now.

Hey, that's not a bad lineup. Maybe I'm pretty good at physical self-care—kind of awesome, actually. They reflect lots of principles 1, 2, and 6: *Self-care is a daily, lifelong practice; Self-care is self-love;* and *Self-care must be realistic to be effective.* I know some of these twenty items might look like treats or indulgences, and not the meat and potatoes (or rather the kale and multivitamins) of self-care. But this mix of habits is, for me, beautifully sustainable. The perfume, the baths, and the candles all count. They all send the message to myself that I matter and am worth taking care of.

Our Physical Self-Care Needs Change Over Time

As I compiled that list, though, I discovered there were things that I used to do regularly for physical self-care that I no longer do. I used to run every morning, do Pilates three times a week, and monitor my protein intake. As I review the changes I made, some of them a bit compromised in the White Magic self-care category, I find that instead of feeling guilty, I have a more self-caring response. I am coming to discover that my former overly strict physical self-care rules were not responsive to my real needs and not always good for me. My knees hurt from all that running, and I injured my shoulder during Pilates, but I kept pushing through.

I also see that, as with all self-care, my needs changed along with whatever challenges I was facing. Right after I left my marriage, running was major self-care for me. It was a moving meditation, a nervous-energy dispeller, and a physical reminder that I can and will get through hard times and feel better for it. When I started my own therapy practice, I was doing Pilates, getting massages, and seeing a chiropractor—all things that might sound like treats—because of the back and leg pain that came with sitting too much. Now that I'm not dealing with those same stressors, I have modified my self-care accordingly.

My middle-aged body no longer finds running to be what it needs, and so I don't run. I miss those endorphins, and I could ignore the reality that my knees don't like running, but it would be at my own peril to do so. In all self-care, we can modify and adapt to our current needs. Take the time to discover what your body needs now. You need not base your physical self-care on rules, dictums, or the latest nutrition fads.

Finally, as I look at my self-care assessment, I come to a sense of self-forgiveness. In my earlier, unrealistic expectations, I felt that my only option for grade-A physical self-care was to be working out two hours a day, meditating, and cooking healthy meals. That's such a narrow measure of physical self-care, and yet, when I wasn't doing those things, I felt like a failure. Forget my rocking inventory of pretty high-level self-care—without the big workouts, I thought I was a failure. But exercising in that way simply doesn't speak to what I need right now. Instead, I've found ways to modify my exercise routine so it meets my current needs. I can say with pride that I take very good care of my body.

Let's close with an example of the healing powers of physical self-care. A young mother named Sumiko told me about a difficult time in her life—and how a painful, fraught self-care practice in her past has become a joyful ritual today.

My son was a colicky baby who wanted no one but me, and I was exhausted. On top of that, my partner had checked out emotionally and wanted nothing to do with our child. At the end of the day, I'd ask him to hold our son while I showered quickly. Just please hold him, I'd say— don't put him in the bouncer to scream and cry. Please engage him. In response, I got an eye roll and a terse Fine. My heart would sink and I'd rush guiltily through my shower. Eventually, I started showering late at night. It cost me precious sleep, but it was better than asking his father for help. Sometimes I barely got three showers a week.

That was three years ago, and my partner finally left us. Because of that period in my life, I now take the longest showers in the world. I use hair product I would have never dreamed of buying before. As I use it, I am telling myself, "I love you. You are good enough, smart enough, pretty enough; you are enough as you are; and you deserve to take care of yourself." Every pump of my beautifying oil is a gift to myself. I use it in my son's hair, too. He doesn't realize the significance of it, as he's four, but it's my small way of showing him he is worthy too. Oh, and I let him take his own ridiculously long baths!

Through these rituals, Sumiko empowers herself with self-care. (Remember principles 1 and 2: *Self-care is a daily, lifelong practice* and *Self-care is self-love.*)

And even better, small actions, like Sumiko's showers, remind us that we don't have to look to others as our only source of love. If we continually send the message to ourselves that we are worthy of care and tending, those beliefs will seep into what we tolerate in work, relationships, and beyond. And that's what we'll focus on in the next chapter.

But first let's do a self-quiz on your physical self-care. That will put you in a good spot to make whatever changes you need.

There is no *one right way* to take care of your beautiful, unique, idiosyncratic, and ever-changing body.

SELF-QUIZ

Your Physical Self-Care

1. What are your White Magic physical self-care beliefs—the rules that you believe you *should* follow to take care of your body? Name them: get them all down in black and white. Notice how some rules may contradict each other. How many of your rules you are living up to? This is not to judge; this is about noticing. What are your rules in the following areas?

   - food/nutrition
   - water intake
   - movement/exercise
   - stress-relieving activities
   - medical and dental care
   - clothing
   - grooming (hair, skin, makeup, bathing)
   - touch/sex/physical pleasure
   - sound (music, nature, other sounds)
   - safety issues (how do you keep yourself safe?)

2. How do your expectations about perfection and/or strict rules allow you to engage in all-or-nothing thinking?

3. If you were to be more flexible, or less flexible, in your self-care style, what changes might you make to your practice? Would you let your-

self be more (or less) adaptable? Where might you move the limits of what is acceptable for you?

4. What are you doing for physical self-care? Name it, own it, see it. Again, this is not about judgment; it is just information. By becoming aware of how you are doing self-care, you will become better at it. As we talked about in chapter 4, "You Are Here," you have to know where you are in order to get where you want to go. What are you currently doing for self-care in the following areas?

- food/nutrition
- water intake
- movement/exercise
- stress-relieving activities
- medical and dental care
- clothing
- grooming (hair, skin, makeup, nails)
- touch/sex/physical pleasure
- sound (music, nature, other sounds)
- safety issues (how do you keep yourself safe?)

5. What safety and health issues are you responding to in a neglectful or indulgent style? This is your one precious body; how are you treating it in a way that doesn't reflect that fact?

6. In what ways are you giving yourself Gray Magic self-care in the physical category that could be improved a bit and dealt with more directly? Examples:

- I am tired, but instead of sleeping more, I drink more coffee.
- I get massages because my back kills me, but I never exercise, and I sit in an uncomfortable chair at my desk.
- I eat a candy bar instead of lunch.
- I work for three straight hours without drinking water because if I drank anything, I'd have to get up and pee.

- I squint and get headaches when I work, but I haven't seen an eye doctor because I know glasses will be expensive.

- I'm putting on weight, but I don't have time to prepare healthy food.

- I've had a cough for three weeks, but I hate going to the doctor with all those sick people.

- Chocolate gives me migraines, but I can't say no to my co-worker at her birthday party or my friend at her baby shower.

7. Are you using any Black Magic methods of self-care? If so, what resources can help you recover from these attempts at destructive self-care?

Caring for Yourself in Relationships

Partners, Family, Friends, and Others

My mom always used to say "You can't say I love you before you can say I."
And I think that sort of makes sense.

—Mindy Kaling

IT'S ALL WELL AND GOOD to care for your mind and body, to be a self-care master in those domains, but if you aren't taking care of yourself in relationship to other people, you're missing some major opportunities. It may seem counterintuitive, but self-care happens in the midst of a variety of relationships—with lovers, spouses, family members, friends, co-workers, even strangers. We live in a world of relationships. Even if you don't have a primary relationship or have no family, once you leave your home, you are in relationship with others. (One could argue that even total recluses don't exist in a vacuum, although their relationships may be on hold to some degree.) And within all of those relationships, self-care can make all the difference. That's what this chapter is all about.

We'll focus here on the most common relationship realities: patterns that don't serve us, learning to stand up for our needs, recognizing relationships that nurture us and those that deplete us. **Note:** If your relationships are difficult and complex, please seek professional help. Abusive relationships, long-standing family dysfunctions, substance abuse, or partnerships on the verge of collapse: if you are having any of these issues, please see a professional therapist as soon as possible.

Oh! And if you *are* living like a recluse . . . here's your chance to come down from the mountaintop. Avoiding relationships takes a lot of work and energy. If you're going to that much effort, my hunch is that you have some baggage about relationships and are withdrawing in a wonky attempt at self-care: "I've been hurt and let down, so I moved to a mountaintop to protect myself from more hurt." If this is you, I hope that the self-care strategies in this chapter will bring you down from the clouds. The view from up there may be nice, but you're missing out on the fulfillment and joy that meaningful relationships can provide—messy as they sometimes are—and I'd like to welcome you back to give it another try.

We Learn about Self-Care through Our First Relationships

Everything we learn about self-care comes initially through those very important relationships with the people who raised us and other key authority figures in our lives. What they did, how they felt (about us and about themselves), and what they said (and what they didn't say) taught us whether our most basic feelings and needs were affirmed or experienced as a burden. We learned whether open communication was encouraged or restricted, whether boundaries were respected or ignored, and in the end, whether we could trust ourselves and others. You may not be able to articulate what you learned about self-care in childhood, but uncovering what you've internalized from those experiences will help guide you to better self-care today.

If we weren't properly nurtured as a baby and young child, we internalize that neglect as the sense that *I am not worth it,* and we learn to neglect ourselves. As adults, we may remain trapped in what Carl Jung called the "child archetype," living in hope that if we don't take care of ourselves, maybe other people finally will. The unspoken fear underlying this choice might be expressed this way: "If I start to take care of myself, then I lose the chance of ever being taken care of by another." The sad paradox is that when we wait for another person to take care of us without making our needs known, we are neglecting ourselves, and our needs continue to go unmet.

In my therapy practice, I've seen many people who are frustrated, hurt, and enraged that they didn't get what they needed from their parents, and who then choose to neglect themselves. Rarely, if ever, do people end up getting what they want by this method—and believe me, I know; I tried it myself long ago. Sometimes, by totally refusing to do the basics of self-care, we might fall apart so completely that we make it necessary for people to show up to rescue us. This desperate situation rarely creates the kind of warm, fuzzy supportive experience we hoped for. Rather, we typically end up feeling like stunted children, ashamed and guilty about accepting the kind of care more appropriate for a three-year-old.

Patterns: How the Past Informs Our Present Relationships

The extra tricky part about the impact of this early care (or lack of it) is that as kids we were totally dependent on these adults; if they chose not to care for us, we would have been helpless. Now, in adult relationships with adult interdependencies, we might start to feel that same helpless panic and irrationally project that fear onto the other person: "My life depends upon you taking care of my needs." But as adults, we are now supposed to be able to take care of ourselves. We have the tools—or can go about getting the tools—that allow us to be responsible for keeping ourselves safe and well. There is freedom in that, but there is also some loss in it: we are no longer a three-year-old who can expect other people to meet our every need. This means we may have some grieving to do and need to work toward accepting the hard fact that, as an adult, our care is now, for the most part, up to us.

Sometimes we try to unconsciously re-create the family dynamics of our childhood, not because they were necessarily good dynamics, but because they are familiar. In an effort to see the present in the same way that we see the past, we may pick partners and friends who prove our worldview. We may not even know it's possible to have relationships that are different from the ones we had with our parents and other caregivers. Long-trodden patterns are not so easy to overcome. It takes time to relearn that, yes, we have needs and that these needs can be met in healthy ways as adults in our current relationships.

For years, for example, I kept finding myself in relationships with men who were various versions of my father—charming but aloof, funny but critical, and who had little time for or interest in me. Once I figured out what I was doing, I tried picking someone who was the exact opposite of my father. At the time, that seemed like major progress, but now I see that I was still using my father as a benchmark. Similarly, a wise therapist once tried to tell me that turning right because my parents turned left was not freedom, but it took me years to learn this lesson. This is, for me, still a work in progress.

The truth is that because of my family history, if I'm not vigilant, I tend to expect that when I have a need, it will go unmet. Although I know this is not a healthy worldview, I can still revert to it, and it comes up in my life all the time. I am far from alone in this pattern. In my role as a therapist, I help people overcome the unhealthy patterns and lessons they learned in childhood, and it is shocking how many of them revolve around this basic idea of asking for what you need. Let's explore what this looks like—and how to recognize and replace these patterns with healthier ones that foster self-care.

One common pattern: We don't ask for what we want

Here's a scenario that still happens all too frequently in my life. My partner, Keith, asks me a simple question, such as "Where do you want to go to eat?" or "What do you want to do on Saturday?" and I say, "I don't know" or "It doesn't matter."

Is it always true that I don't know what I want to eat or what I want to do? Of course not. But there are old tapes from childhood in my head that tell me things like this: *Don't be selfish. Let him choose. You don't want to be a bother. Men like women who defer to their wants and needs.* And some of my past relationships confirmed this message; when I asked for what I wanted, I'd get an audible sigh, or I'd be told, "Sorry, that's inconvenient." So my automatic thought is often *better to keep your needs to yourself.* I hate to admit that, but it's true, and sometimes those thoughts still have the power to stop me. Lessons learned in childhood can be hard to shake.

In the five years I've been with Keith, my asking for something has never led to a disappointment or argument. Nonetheless, I have to soothe and remind myself before I ask: *I know that Keith has never gotten upset with me for asking for what I want. This is old stuff with other people that makes me nervous. It is going to be fine. Keith loves me and he likes doing things for me.* And then I can express my needs, and everything works out. You might imagine that after five years I wouldn't need to keep soothing myself this way, but my time with Keith is less than 10 percent of my life. The old neural wiring has been around a whole lot longer.

For me and for many of the clients I treat, there is another layer to our reluctance to ask for what we want: we had a caretaker with a narcissistic personality disorder. Narcissists generally feel entitled to everything, expecting their needs to be the center of attention. They often express themselves in a grandiose fashion that can be cringe-worthy. With that example of how to ask for what we want, we may conclude that it is simply better not to ask for much of anything.

So how do we grow from passive child to active adult? Let's trace the whole chronology. It begins with this super short period when everything you wanted came to you. It was wonderful. You were hungry and there was food. You were tired and you slept. You needed to poop and pee, and you just did it. You knew no major irritation or delay between need and fulfillment. It was heaven—or rather it was pre-birth and a few magic moments between you and Mom after your birth. When you came fully into this world, all of a sudden your needs weren't met so instantly and easily, and then you cried. You grew up a bit and you started to use words. You would, on occasion, ask for things like cookies for breakfast or a Barbie Dream House, and you started to hear that horrible word *no*, and it sucked. At times you longed for that perfect, blissful time where all your needs were met without your having to ask. In essence, you thought, *If they loved me, they would just know what I want. If I ask, it ruins it.*

But as you developed cognitive and verbal skills, and then emerged from adolescence and into young adulthood, you realized that while that may be a nice dream, you left the Eden of immediate gratification long ago. Growing up means taking the responsibility of communicating our needs—or staying at the infantile level of expecting others to guess what we need and magically fulfill it. As mature adults, we have varied needs and wants. We can't expect others to guess them, nor can we guess theirs. Learning to ask for what you need from the people around you is a powerful step toward taking responsibility for your self-care through fostering healthy, supportive adult relationships.

It's taken time and a lot of work, but I have learned this lesson well—and so can you. It doesn't have to be dramatic or complicated, and it often plays out in the simplest everyday interactions. Just today I had lots of opportunities for self-care in relationships:

- When Keith brought me coffee, I asked for a hug as well.
- When he asked how I wanted to spend my Saturday night, I told him.
- I reached out to a friend for some support via text.
- I ended my workday on time.
- I met a friend for dinner, and for bonus points, we had an emotionally honest and vulnerable conversation, where I dared to tell her how I felt when it might have been easier not to do so. (And I chose not to check my phone while we were together.)
- I got support and encouragement from that friend.

On other days, I have asked others for help in many small ways: errands, dog care, brainstorm sessions, and so on. I have also hired coaches and therapists to support me during times of transition. In other words, I've questioned my childhood "lessons" about keeping my needs and wants to myself. I've replaced them with new lessons that allow me to take responsibility for making my needs known and building nurturing relationships that support self-care. I wish the same for you.

It's not enough just to ask for help and get our needs met in our relationships. We also need to be able to speak our truth. This can manifest itself in many ways depending on the relationship, but at its roots, it's about being honest with yourself about what you believe and what you need on a soul level—which is another way of saying that we need to be clear about our expectations. The better we can communicate those needs and also be clear whether or not those needs are being met, the more satisfying our relationships are going to be.

When We Abandon Ourselves in Relationships

When we neglect ourselves, we can't be our best selves, and that has an undeniable cost to our relationships. The more we take care of our mind, body, spirit, and possessions, the less likely we'll expect another person to do it for us. That "other people make me whole" myth? Yes, it was good for romantic effect in the film *Jerry Maguire* when the Tom Cruise character said the famous line "You complete me" to the character played by Renée Zellweger. But *other people don't complete you.* They can't. *You* complete you. If you enter a relationship believing that myth, you risk losing yourself and putting an impossible burden on the other person—a burden that will eventually kill the romance and possibly the relationship itself.

Looking for someone to complete you is what I call "one-stop shopping for love." We seek a romantic partner who can be our best friend and lover, playmate, accountant, wardrobe consultant, and therapist—and guess what: no one can ever be all those things to another person. Our desire to abandon our identity in a relationship and find someone to "complete us" leads to social isolation and frustration, since no one can ever be all things to anyone else. Our self-care relationship needs are met not just through our intimate partners, but also through friends, family, acquaintances, co-workers, and even service providers. It cannot be one person's job to take care of all of your needs; it is too much to expect, and it guarantees disappointment.

When parents lose themselves to their kids

When people become parents, they tend to abandon themselves in that role. I think back to my own mother. She took care of my dad, me, her home, and her business: "Resort wear doesn't sell itself," she used to say. But time for her? Time to ask herself what she needed? Not so much. Truth be told, I barely remember my mother even *sitting*; she was always a whirling dervish of domestic activity, all while running a successful retail clothing business. Self-care was not something she valued or made time for. She had, in other words, abandoned herself in her family role.

When I was in grade school, my mother took me along to her hair-coloring appointments at the Jon Peters Salon in Beverly Hills. I loved seeing my mother in a glamorous salon sipping coffee under the care of a hairdresser to the stars. I couldn't have told you why, but it made me happy to see my mother taking care of herself.

Then one day when I was about ten, all that changed. My mother announced that she was no longer going to color her hair: she was going natural. I was crestfallen. It wasn't just that she'd be the only gray-haired mom in my elementary school—there was something deeper than that. I had a hunch that my mother was *happier* after her salon pampering. I begged her not to stop coloring her hair.

At about the same time, I became friends with two neighborhood girls and met their glamorous divorcée mother, Frances. She was a successful businesswoman with a boyfriend who seemed to love her. Unlike my mom, Frances was very much into her own self-care. Her long brown hair looked like a Breck advertisement; she was always well dressed; she padded around the house in a brown silk kimono and chic little slippers with marabou feather trim. Her bedroom looked like a sanctuary of rest and sensuality: the vanity with its potions and perfumes, the elegant bed with its brown faux fur blanket. I studied her and decided I wanted to be just like Frances when I grew up. Again, I didn't know what I meant by that. I thought I just liked all the pretty things. And, yes, the aesthetics of Frances's world were beautiful, but again, I wanted something deeper.

I loved that Frances somehow managed to take care of herself *and* be a mother. She showed me that self-care is powerful, and it impacts how others treat you. I think my Frances crush was obvious to my mother and may have seemed silly to her. But what I wanted for myself, my mother, and now for you, dear reader, is to know that caring for others doesn't have to mean self-neglect. People whom you care for benefit from and are inspired by your own self-care.

Today, I see a lot of parents in my practice, particularly moms, who behave exactly the way my mom did. In fact, with 24/7 connectivity, it's even worse. Parents are always on, and it is all too easy for them to lose themselves to their families and to work. Sometimes, they even mention it with pride, saying, "My husband and I never go on dates without the kids" or "I haven't spent a night away from my son since he was born." That's not healthy for anyone.

If this is you, take the time to assess your self-care needs. Start with some Gray Magic self-care (see chapter 3) and work up to some of the White Magic.

The alternative—abandoning yourself to your family or work—isn't in the best interest of anyone involved.

My friend Karen Cohen is a fellow therapist and a mother of two young daughters. She wrote a letter that she imagined an overscheduled, self-care-denying parent might write to a newborn. It speaks to the risk parents take when they ignore their own needs.

Dear Sweet Little One,

I feel so blessed that we will be sharing our lives together and that I will have the supreme privilege of being your parent. I thought I would write down my dreams for your future.

I hope you will eat poorly and sporadically so that your cholesterol is elevated and you don't have a lot of energy. I hope your eating habits will lead to a sedentary life so you will always struggle with an extra ten to twenty pounds. As you get busier, I want you to not make time to call and keep up with special friends so that when difficulties come in life, and they will, you will have no one to reach out to or to ask for support. Be sure that you do not go to the doctor or dentist often enough to create a strong and trusting relationship so if you ever confront an illness, you will have a stranger to offer you medical advice, and you won't know if their advice is sound because you have no history with them.

Let your looks slide, wear out-of-date clothes, and don't put effort into your environment. I hope you forget to make special time for your partner because you take care of everyone else in life and your relationship becomes stale and you feel like strangers. I want you to be bored and stressed in life because you never take the time to think about what interests you or to try new things. I will try to ensure these dreams come true for you by modeling this every single day of my life so that you will know just how to make this happen. I love you that much.

Love,

Mommy

That's a letter no one in the history of parenting ever wanted to send to their kids. Truly loving your children means taking care of yourself well enough that you can take good care of them.

Basic Expectations in Significant Relationships

We all hold many expectations of our closest relationships, some essential and some more mundane. "I expect to be treated well and with respect" is basic. But we may have other everyday expectations that we allow to go unmet, pretending we don't really care. Simple things such as your partner offering verbal praise when you've accomplished something, making spontaneous displays of affection, giving you their full attention when you're talking, asking about your day, or remembering your birthday (and maybe even making you a cake!). When we pretend that we don't really want to have those needs met and don't make our expectations known, we're not practicing good self-care.

In therapy, people seem to love to tell me that they're done with having expectations. My reaction? I tell them that denying expectations doesn't make them go away; it simply pushes them into the murky unconscious, where they will fester and cause you to fume with disappointment and anger. Rather than eventually expressing your frustration through "I deserve" outbursts, it is far better to know your expectations, name them, and befriend them. Let them all out into the light of day! Show yourself in all your needy glory. You still may not get all those little expectations met by that significant person—remember, no one person can "complete you." But once you know what your needs are, it is absolutely possible to either meet them yourself or bring people into your life who can help you meet them.

For example, my family never gave me the rah-rah encouragement I wanted, and so I stopped expecting it. Later in life, I realized I really, really love to be encouraged (and to encourage others), so I've gathered an incredible group of friends who are the most boisterous cheerleaders this side of Texas.

Know When to Fold and When to Stay

Which relationships add to your quality of life, and which deplete you? That awareness is super important in self-care. Obviously, it seems wise not to hang with people who make you feel bad about yourself—but it's not always that simple. All relationships have some negative and some positive charge, and when you can't completely avoid the negative, you can compensate with added self-care. For example, you aren't going to stop visiting your grandmother in the nursing home simply because it depresses you. Likewise, you can't stop talking to your mother just because she calls you three times a day, even though you've told her once a week would be plenty. And maybe you have to see your hypercritical father-in-law on certain holidays. Some relationships you can't kick to the curb. Some you make your peace with because they offer more positives than negatives in the long run.

Sometimes these relationships call for extra self-care measures. Sarah's mother-in-law often calls her at work, telling her secretary it's an emergency when it's really something benign, like asking if she'd seen a particular movie. Finally, Sarah got a separate phone line just for her mother-in-law, and now all her messages go to this line's voice mail. Sarah told me, "This seems like an extreme measure, but she wouldn't stop calling, and I had to do something. My work was suffering with all her interruptions."

Kiki describes how she approaches tough family situations. "I arm myself with this strangely comforting motto: *There is no winning in my family,*" she says. "I know that doesn't sound like a comfort, but it is; it takes me out of thinking that what I do or don't do will make a difference. The truth is there are people in my family who don't want to be happy, and you can't make people happy who don't want to be happy."

When dealing with difficult people, ask yourself if your expectations are reasonable, and if so, what you might do to get them met. If there is no way, at least you know. In that case, simply figure out the good you're getting from these relationships and then go for that. What can be reasonably expected? Does Aunt Anita make a mean carrot cake even if she's a bit cranky? Can you enjoy the stories your hypercritical father-in-law tells? Are your sister's insufferable dinner parties always hosted in a beautiful environment with the best of intentions? Yes, you'd like more from these relationships than cakes, stories, and nice interior design, but that may not be possible. So plan around it, enjoy it as best you can, and then give yourself some extra self-care afterward.

When to walk away

Self-care can't always fix what's wrong in a relationship. Some relationships injure us and deplete us to the point of toxicity, and in those cases, no amount of self-care will make them bearable. Sometimes you simply have to walk away from people, even those who have meant a lot to you in the past. If you are being physically and emotionally abused, if you are chronically being mistreated, if the other person won't admit that something is wrong and that they need to change, self-care is not going to make things better. The most self-caring choice might be to let go of the relationship, knowing it will be painful, and get the help you need to deal with the pain you've been through and then move on.

• • •

There is a lot of self-care to do in relationships: understanding what the past is telling you about your needs and relationships, learning to ask for what you need, speaking your truth, not abandoning yourself, allowing yourself expectations, and knowing when to walk away. Mastering these lessons can take a lifetime, but they're not the only work you need to do in your relationships. You have a powerful, versatile skill just waiting to be developed. It's called setting boundaries, and it's what we'll discuss in the next chapter. Hold on to your hat—because learning how to set boundaries in your relationships is going to bring powerful change to your life.

It's not enough just to ask for help and
get our needs met in our relationships.
We also need to be able to speak our truth.

SELF-QUIZ

Self-Care in Your Relationships

1. What did your relationship with your parents teach you about relationships?

2. How do you ask for what you need in relationships? What don't you ask others for that you need?

3. How do you abandon yourself in relationships?

4. How does caring for yourself improve your relationships?

5. How do you abandon your self-care in the name of caring for others?

6. What could you be communicating to your kids by not caring for yourself?

7. What could you communicate to your kids by caring for yourself?

8. What expectations do you have of your relationships? Are those expectations met?

9. Which relationships add to the quality of your life?

10. Which relationships drain you?

11. In past relationships, how have you known when it was time to walk away?

CHAPTER EIGHT

The Beauty of Boundaries

Self-Care Skills for Relationships

*Setting boundaries is a way of caring for myself. It doesn't make me mean,
selfish, or uncaring because I don't do things your way. I care about me too.*

—Christine Morgan

SIMPLY CARING FOR OURSELVES is challenging enough in today's
world, but self-care in the context of relationships adds many layers of complexity, as we saw in chapter 8. Now I have good news for you. There's a special skill that will help you navigate that complexity. It will build your own
self-respect and others' respect for you. It will give you guideposts in your relationships and help prevent feelings of resentment and craziness. This chapter
is all about boundaries: setting them, protecting them, and respecting others'
boundaries, too. As a bonus, we'll also discuss two closely related skills: saying
no and getting over always being so damn nice.

Remember principle 3? *Self-care means taking personal responsibility.* Here's
our chance to rise to a challenge—one that we (and only we) can do something about. So let's flex our boundary-setting muscles and get started.

The Art of Boundaries

In therapy, the concept of boundaries is a biggie. Drawing on a sports metaphor, we speak of setting and observing boundaries in relationships. Behavior
that we deem acceptable is "within bounds" in our relationships, and what we

consider unacceptable is totally "out of bounds." We need to know what we will tolerate—physically, psychologically, and mentally—and what we won't with our friends, family, and romantic partners. Boundaries allow us to differentiate ourselves from each other. They communicate identity: "I am me, and my needs, desires, and expectations differ from yours, and I am willing to voice them."

Our boundaries might be rigid, loose, somewhere in between, or even nonexistent. A complete lack of boundaries may indicate that we don't have a strong identity or are enmeshed with someone else. That narrative goes like this: "It doesn't matter what I want; I only want what *you* want."

Boundaries are not just about what behaviors we accept; they are also about how much we are open or closed to others. If we grew up in a family where there were no boundaries—no private space, no ability to say no, no doors shut, nothing respected as private property, or, worst of all, physical and sexual abuse—we may have developed overly strict or rigid boundaries to protect ourselves. That makes sense. But if we're so closed off that we're like a locked vault, then we're too guarded and defensive to make connections with other people. If, on the other hand, we're a totally open book with no secrets, limits, or personal space, then being around others will leave us feeling depleted, drained, and lacking in a solid sense of self. Rigid boundaries are definitely appropriate in certain categories: abuse, for example, is *never* okay, ever. In other categories, however, some flexibility around boundaries is necessary and totally healthy. In short, super-firm boundaries can be as unhealthy as loosey-goosey boundaries. Again, it depends on context. Remember principle 5: *Self-care requires attention and responsiveness.*

What might it sound like to declare a boundary? Here are some examples of clear, practical boundaries that could help keep relationships in good working order:

- I am not okay with my husband talking to his ex-girlfriend.
- I need my kids to tell me when they're going to be home late.
- I feel disrespected when you don't listen or you interrupt me when I'm speaking.
- I expect you to pay back the money you borrowed.

- When you borrow my stuff, I expect you to return it in working order.
- It is not okay with me for my roommates to go in my room without my permission.
- I expect my friends to not repeat personal information that I share with them.
- I expect my partner to discuss large purchases with me before he makes them.
- If a door is shut, I expect my family members to knock before entering.
- It is absolutely not okay for porn to be in our home.
- It is definitely not okay for men other than my husband to be affectionate or flirty toward me.
- Don't call me at work unless it is an emergency.
- I am not okay with you commenting on my body, weight, or appearance.
- I expect my partner to share information with me that affects our relationship or my well-being.
- Do not call me after 9 p.m.
- It is not okay for you to blare music before I get up in the morning.
- I get to decide what kind of touch, sexuality, and contact I have with others.
- No, I am not interested in/not ready for a sexual relationship with you.
- I will not have sex without a condom.
- I don't want to be tagged in Facebook photos.
- I am not okay with you writing about our relationship on social media.
- I know I said I could do that favor for you, but I am not able to.

Why setting boundaries is so hard

You might believe that love is never having to set boundaries, but that's wrong. You might believe that love requires us to deny our own needs, but that is also wrong. You might have learned that endless giving is what being a mother, wife, or friend is all about, and you may feel guilty at the mere notion of setting a boundary. Self-care challenges that idea. Self-care says that we have an absolute requirement to not let ourselves be stepped on.

You might feel setting a boundary is not worth the risk because of the anger or conflict that could arise from doing so. But in my practice and personal experience, this is absolutely not true. As Dr. Henry Cloud and Dr. John Townsend wrote in their book *Boundaries,* "The person who is angry at you for setting boundaries is the one with the problem. . . . Maintaining your boundaries is good for other people; it will help them learn what their families of origin did not teach them: to respect other people."[15]

Reflecting on my own life, I am super good about my boundaries in some areas. Give me a gold star in my work life. I take Sundays off, I won't take calls after 9 p.m., I keep sessions to fifty minutes, and I charge for sessions not canceled twenty-four hours in advance. In my personal life, too, there are some boundaries that I am firm and absolute about. I will only be in relationships with people who are supportive, honest, and respectful. I absolutely will not tolerate physical abuse. My friends are respectful of my boundaries regarding when I am available to chat, and they know that my Sundays are spent with my significant others.

But that being said, boundaries have been a challenge for me throughout my life. I often have an automatic reaction to avoid conflict. As a result, I will sometimes know exactly what my boundary is but do not dare to verbalize it. Then, if someone "ignores" that unexpressed boundary—totally blamelessly—I feel screamingly violated, yet I don't object; nobody but me knows about it because I'd never communicated the boundary. I experience the anger and resentment of a boundary violation, but I never set it to begin with. The problem, in this case, is mine.

Or perhaps I've set a boundary, but it's been crossed. When someone metaphorically tracks their dirty boots over my "No you don't" zone, I feel shocked. I know I am not okay with what has just happened, but I fear that confronting the person will lead to a fight. And I believe that I don't know how to fight without getting hurt. I feel creepy and awful that a boundary has been violated and even worse that—unlike the umpires at Wimbledon, who so loudly call "out!"—I didn't confront it. I have a bad feeling in my stomach. That somatic sensation tells me I am going to be in big trouble if I say, "No! Not okay! Out of bounds!" so I stuff the feeling and suffer in silence.

In reflecting on my own boundaries and why I don't set them and then stick to them, it comes down to a sense that I'm somehow undeserving. But I am *entitled* to boundaries. As soon as something goes into my out-of-bounds zone—even a clearly declared one—my nervous system tells me there is little to nothing I can do about it. I don't feel entitled to defend that boundary. I fear that the other person would be angry, maybe irrationally so, if I tried. I feel hopeless; I take no action.

I am not alone in this syndrome. I hear about boundary guilt a lot in my work, especially from women. Here are the myths that most often stop us from setting or protecting our boundaries:

- I am wrong to need boundaries.
- If I set boundaries, they won't be respected.
- If I set boundaries, I will lose love.
- Love doesn't need boundaries.

Monica—who we met earlier in this book—struggles with some of those myths. A loving and attentive mother, she sheepishly reports that she'll do anything for her kids, rarely enforcing consequences when they overstep the rules. She can't stand feeling like her kids are angry at her, so she avoids confronting them—in fact, she's weak on setting clear schedules and expectations. She fears that if she asserts her boundaries, her kids won't love her. "I never take time for myself," she says, "even though their having a consistent bedtime would mean so much to me. I could take time for Pilates and chatting with friends. I know it would help me be a better mother if I took that time for myself, but I feel so guilty saying no to a request for another story."

Monica sees how her own childhood set her up for this behavior. "I had a narcissistic mother," she told me. "Everything was run by her needs, and she was extremely entitled about her needs. She could never be pleased. Whatever you gave her was never enough and always the wrong kind. As a kid, I spent most of my time trying to clean up my mom's messes. She would act like the Queen of Sheba with salespeople, waitresses, and everyone, so I would compensate for her—I would be super nice and accommodating and overly grateful. And so when people cross my boundaries, I feel like I have to be nice, unlike my mom. I don't say anything, because I fear that I will be attacked for saying my boundary has been crossed."

Monica has the insight she needs. Now she just needs to take action.

HOW FEAR STOPS PEOPLE FROM SETTING BOUNDARIES

I know people who are afraid of antiques, moths, hair products, salad bars, and even egg yolks. All of those fears, I suppose, have their own logic. But a fear of anger seems, to my mind, wise—wiser even than a fear of public speaking or heights. And those of us with a history of trauma have to work especially hard to overcome fear of anger. Setting boundaries can be a trigger for those who grew up in homes where boundaries weren't allowed or were chaotic and ever changing. So we might not set boundaries as a way to avoid an expectation from the past. The thinking goes like this: "If I set boundaries, Dad got mad at me, and so I believe all people will get mad at me for having boundaries." That, my friend, is a cognitive distortion—an expectation that what happened in the past is going to happen again. The difference between then and now is that you aren't a kid, and if someone doesn't respect your boundaries, you get to do very adult things like say, "Get lost." You can leave, enlist help, call the cops if needed. If someone doesn't respect you and your boundaries, you can choose self-respect, choose self-care, and move on.

I shared with my wise boundary-setting guru of a friend, Pammy, that I needed to set some boundaries but wasn't able to do so, that I was afraid of how the persons in question would respond. They would surely attack me, yell, scream, and tell me I am stupid and ugly. Irrational? Yes. Does that irrational fear stop me and silence me? Absolutely.

Upon hearing my irrational inner dialogue, Pammy said, "I have an assignment for you. I want you to report to me any and all instances when you set a boundary and the other person gets angry at you. But in the moment when it happens, I want you to become aware of your anger that comes up and let it out, not in a crazy rage-filled way—but in a way that gives voice to that anger. If your boundaries aren't being respected, then use your body, your energy, or your words to tell that person to *back off*. I want you to report back to me."

I nervously agreed, and just a week later I had an opportunity to practice. I was meeting with a woman who became completely disrespectful and confrontational. I knew for sure that I was not okay with how she was treating me. I self-talked my way through it and thought, *This person already sees me as difficult and problematic, so what have I got to lose? There's no reason not to stand up for myself.* Now, for the record, let me tell you, I was scared. My legs were shaking. I was uncomfortable. I was sure I was going to get in "big trouble" (when that phrase occurs to me, it's code that I've time-traveled back to being a little girl). I wanted to suppress my anger, but I remembered the assignment that Pammy gave me. So I did it. I confronted the woman who was tap dancing over my boundaries. I got clear, adopted a strong voice, and said, "You are being disrespectful. I am not okay with this."

Amazingly, the woman backed down, though I still felt a bit of that shaky "big trouble" feeling, worried that she might see me as "not nice." But mostly I felt relieved that I had set the boundary and now had some new hope of resolution and change. I self-soothed and told myself this uncomfortable feeling would pass and that I deserved to set the boundary. And I thought about what Pammy said: "If there is somebody who is going to be hurt in a situation where I have a boundary, it is not going to be me." While to the boundaryless that might sound harsh, those who are starting to recognize what lacking boundaries costs the self and relationships can see the wisdom of my friend's words.

After I did the scary boundary setting and lived to tell the tale, I did it again the same week in another situation. And I'm finding it gets easier each time. I still feel a bit awkward at the moment I speak up to set or defend a boundary, especially if I fear anger or being seen as not nice. But it feels so good to have the boundary set that I am now willing to go through the awkward moments to get to the good part: changed behavior and clearer air. Certainly, some people have not been thrilled with my boundaries—plenty of people wanted me to stay being nice, and some were so upset with my newfound power that the relationship broke apart. I had been so afraid of that reality, but the truth is that I don't want to be in relationships that prohibit me from having boundaries.

The cost of too-loose or nonexistent boundaries

We may be paying a price for the boundaries we fail to set. According to *Boundaries* authors Cloud and Townsend, if you have an interaction with someone that leaves you feeling sad, angry, depressed, critical, withdrawn, perfectionistic, and argumentative, it might indicate that a boundary has been crossed. This hurts not only you, but also your relationships.[16] When boundaries are crossed, either knowingly or unknowingly, resentment happens, and when a crust of resentment builds up over time, we can stop feeling love, safety, and all the other warm, ooey-gooey good feelings that come with healthy relationships. These negative feelings can lead to withdrawal, emotional disconnect, and relationship breakdown.

When people fail to directly address boundary violations, their feelings about the violations don't simply disappear. Rather, they come out in other situations. It is common, for example, to get angry about something of little significance. Fights that seem to be about trivial issues—"I can't believe you forgot to buy the milk!"—are merely stand-ins for bigger issues, such as, "I can't count on you to do what you say and say what you mean, and all this distrust is really pissing me off, but I can't say that, so instead I am mad at your forgetting the milk and also at the weird noises you make when you eat . . ." All of this when the real issue was that I am hurt because you disregard my feelings and ignore my requests for intimacy.

Crystal Andrus, author of *The Emotional Edge*, says, "When you feel yourself becoming angry, resentful or exhausted, pay attention to where *you* haven't set a healthy boundary."[17]

WHAT OUR LACK OF BOUNDARIES SAYS TO OTHERS

When people know you have no boundaries, when you communicate the message that you are completely available to them and that you will never say no, they know that you put their needs before yours. Essentially, you are saying that your needs don't matter. If you look like a doormat, act like a doormat, and quack like a doormat (to mix a metaphor), should you shocked by the shoeprints on you? Through your lack of boundary setting, you communicate that you lack self-confidence and self-respect. Strangely, people may come to resent you for your ever-present yes. They may not be able to trust your yes, and they may feel the resentment oozing out behind your mask of "No problem, I don't care that you crashed my car, ate my food, stole my man, and lost my dog." Your behavior is teaching people how to treat you, and you don't want to teach other people that you don't matter. Do you?

Keep working on it. Lots of us struggle with boundaries. "There are some boundaries I am firm about—but lots of other ones I am very loose on," says Vicki, a twenty-three-year-old grad student. "I treat boundaries more like wishes or preferences. I don't protect them because I just can't bear the confrontation that would require. I just couldn't stand having people telling me I am wrong to have a boundary or, after I dared to set one, to have them slop over it again. It seems better not to have them than to have people walk over them. I also notice that I have a big old pile of resentment that comes with me not letting people know my boundaries. I find that I just want to isolate and be on my own. It's tiring to endlessly ignore my needs."

EXAMINE WHAT YOU TOLERATE

If you haven't been setting boundaries, or if they're loosey-goosey, you might not even know what they are. So, before we start on our boundary-setting adventure, first look at all your relationships, including with family, your romantic partner, friends, co-workers, bosses, kids, and strangers, and explore what you are accepting that is making you mad, sad, not-glad, angry, or cuckoo for coconuts. See where you have said yes where you meant no; look at that *ouch* that happens after seeing a certain friend; try to identify what you feel after you see your mother. If you don't know what you are allowing that is causing you hurt, there ain't no way to clean it up. Taking an inventory of each relationship is a good way to start seeing where your boundaries need to get a self-care makeover.

It is obviously essential to know what your boundaries are before you set them. So, what are your absolute truths? Identify a relationship or situation where you need to do some boundary work; then fill in the following blanks. If you are having trouble with this exercise, see Kayla's responses for an example.

I will . . .

I won't . . .

I can't . . .

I am not . . .

I am . . .

I want . . .

I don't want . . .

I have a right to . . .

I need to . . .

To protect myself, I have a right to . . .

My friend Kayla is working on setting boundaries with her alcoholic mother, who brings drama to every encounter. Here are the answers Kayla gave:

KAYLA'S RESPONSES

1. I will remember to tune in to what I want in any encounter with my mother, instead of what I think *she* wants.

2. I won't speak to my mother after 5 p.m. because I can't trust that she will be sober.

3. I can't allow my mother to yell at me or to judge me. I will hang up the phone or walk away if she begins to yell or judge.

4. I am not going to try to make sense of my mother's irrational behavior, because it makes no sense and it saps me of energy to try.

5. I am certain that there is nothing I can do to make my mother happy.

6. I want to stop trying to make my mother happy.

7. I don't want to be more concerned with whether my mother is going to get angry than with whatever I need in any given interaction.

8. I have a right to see my friends when I go home, even if it makes my mother angry.

9. I need to find somewhere else to stay when I visit home. Staying in her house causes me too much pain.

10. To protect myself, I have a right to say no to being together on the next holiday.

Use your words

When you need to express or clarify something—when you are hurt, sad, angry, or disappointed with someone—do you avoid the situation or confront it? Are you verbose, or are words *verboten* when it comes to expressing your ouch? If you aren't using your words but are rather silent-treatmenting it—pouting, displaying dramatic body language, slamming doors, and using other passive-aggressive methods of communication—then people likely aren't getting your drift. You need to do a better job of communicating.

If, on the other hand, you often find yourself embroiled in fights, hurling insults and attacks, then you likely aren't being heard, either. People tend to stop listening when your boundary setting begins with "Hey, you big stupid-head." You want to be heard, and to do that you might need to first figure out exactly what you want to say and how to say it in a way that isn't straight out of the Marcel Marceau miming academy or loaded with the message "Get ready to rumble." You may be trying to say, "I want you to know that I feel crappy, but I don't know how to communicate how I feel," but it is likely the other person isn't getting the message.

Neither extreme is an effective or healthy method of getting your needs met. People don't respond well to them, and even if they get that you aren't happy, they may not know what you want or need, or what the hell you're upset about. It is an act of self-care to say with clarity, "*This* is what I want and *this* is what I don't want. This hurts, and this is why, and I trust that you care about me, so I'm telling you how I feel. I am not blaming you. I just want you to know." Does that sentence feel absolutely impossible to say? Do you have some history in which your needs went unmet? It could be wise to seek professional help to get to the core of why you aren't able to speak your truth around needs and boundaries.

New adventures in boundary setting: A four-step guide

Setting a boundary may be one of the most meaningful acts of self-care you can do. And if you don't feel very good at it, then improving your skills can be more transformative to your self-care than a month-long detox. Like any new skill, boundary setting takes practice, and it may take time for the new boundaries to stick.

Try this four-step guide to boundary setting.

Clarify your intentions.

- Identify the boundary that needs to be set and how you feel about it. Maybe it's already been crossed, or maybe you're identifying it in advance. Decide what you will not tolerate (your husband bringing his cell phone to dinner; inappropriate sexual comments at work). You may want to write this down.

- Notice whether you have set this boundary before with this person; the answer may affect how you communicate it.

- Notice if this is a boundary issue you've had in other relationships; you might gain some insight into the root of the problem.

- Give yourself permission to set a boundary. If you need someone else's permission, take mine. (If you get stuck here, you could delay long enough to get some boundary-setting support: psychotherapy, counseling, and Co-Dependents Anonymous are all useful resources.)

Prepare for the conversation.

- Remind yourself of your exact intention: what do you need to happen, now and in the future, so that the boundary won't be crossed?

- Breathe deeply and ask yourself, *How can I communicate my needs in a way that is kind, respectful, and fair?* I try to channel Martha Stewart. I imagine her boundary setting to be gracious, firm, and clear.

- Get into the mind-set of a person who deserves respect. Try expanding your physical space, feet flat on the floor, to convey a strong identity. (I also soothe the part of me that is freaking out and remind myself of the benefits of boundaries.) Take another deep breath.

Speak up.

- Start with the subject of boundaries in general: "I want both of us to be able to communicate our boundaries to each other." This shows you're open to discussing and honoring the other person's boundaries, too.

- Now say, "This boundary is my attempt at taking care of myself as well as our relationship." This statement communicates that you value the person and is likely to lower defensiveness.

- Next, set the boundary. Say something like, "Boundaries and limits are a healthy part of relationships. I have a boundary of _____ (or *I need* or *I can't do . . .).*" Communicate the boundary clearly.

- If you need to, indicate consequences: "And if you don't respect this boundary, I will _____." Is this scary? Then add this disclaimer: "Setting boundaries is scary for me, and I want you to know that I am doing this because I care so much about our relationship."

- As appropriate, listen to the person's response and discuss the issue.

Recover.

- After the boundary has been set, do some self-care. Call someone who will support the boundary you just set, get some exercise, take a bath, pet your dog, get a hug, use your self-care tools to affirm that you are worth caring for.

As you continue to set boundaries with people and discover that it is okay to have them, you likely won't need to use all of the steps on this list. When your skills improve and you have success at setting and keeping boundaries, you might skip all the preamble and go straight to part 3, "Speak up." You can loosen your tongue with one of these prompts:

This is hard for me to say, but . . .

I have a problem with . . .

I have decided/realized that . . .

I am uncomfortable with . . .

I would rather not . . .

It is unacceptable to me that . . .

It is important to me that . . .

What I need is . . .

I am not all right with . . .

Boundaries can bring clarity and fresh air to a relationship. Flex that boundary-setting muscle and reap the rewards.

Healthy boundary makeovers: Three examples

Let's start with Cara. She realized she needed to set a boundary with a friend who persistently called to talk about her problems, using Cara as a 1-800-DUMP-HERE line. Cara began to feel resentful of the friendship. She dreaded the long phone calls and always felt taken advantage of afterward. She decided to set a boundary. "I hated to do it," says Cara. "I was afraid she was going to be mad at me when I suggested that she needed more help than I could give her as a friend, that she needed a therapist. I even dared to tell her that the relationship had changed to the point where I felt it was all about her, and I was feeling kind of hurt."

As it turned out, Cara was pleasantly surprised by her friend's reaction. "I expected her to yell and scream and tell me I was a horrible friend, but she didn't. I referred her to a therapist. And when she would call again and start to unload on me, forgetting the boundary I set, I would gently remind her that she needed to talk to a therapist, that I couldn't help her with these issues any longer."

Jamila has a sister who seemed to enjoy sharing news about anyone she heard of who had a physical illness or lost a spouse. This was extremely upsetting for Jamila, whose husband had recently had some health scares. So she finally set a boundary and told her sister: "I just can't listen to these endless examples of loss. Please, only tell me about this if it is someone you know directly." Jamila's sister usually stays in the boundaries, and when she doesn't, Jamila reminds her about the request she made. "Now," she explains, "I don't feel resentment as soon as I see that it's my sister calling me. I actually like hearing from her again."

Ava's sister-in-law Rachel was unable to respect her time boundaries. Ava didn't mind babysitting her nieces and nephews, but when Rachel promised to pick up the kids at 7 p.m., Ava couldn't count on that promise. Often, her own plans were railroaded by Rachel's inability to honor her time commitments. Finally, Ava could no longer contain her resentment. First she practiced with her therapist how to set a boundary; then she informed Rachel that she was happy to babysit but only if Rachel could respect her time limitations. At first Rachel was defensive, claiming circumstances beyond her control. Ava acknowledged that of course there would be times like that, but this was a pattern. If Rachel's schedule was not going to change, Ava was no longer going to be able to watch her kids. This time Rachel heard her and hasn't been late since.

What if your boundaries are ignored?

What if you set a boundary in a kind, magnanimous manner and you are met with rage or are told that you are wrong for having a boundary? I know, you were hoping to hear an immediate "Oh my gosh, I had no idea; absolutely, I totally respect your boundary." Well, if you get resistance or defensiveness to your fairly and clearly communicated boundary, there is still room to talk about it. Defensiveness means the person hears they are bad and wrong and they feel attacked; that's where you come back with something like this: "My goal here is not to make you wrong. I want to hear how my boundary around this makes you feel."

But if, after making space for the other's feelings, you can see they have no interest in respecting your boundary, then you have some work to do. It might be time to do some self-care assessment about how you've tolerated mistreatment and what changes you might make in your relationships. When you set a healthy boundary and it is disregarded over and over, that's a red flag. It may indicate that you are in a toxic relationship—or perhaps you already know that. Perhaps you were avoiding setting boundaries because you knew they wouldn't be respected. If this is the case, it might mean doing some scary things, including leaving the relationship. What it certainly *doesn't* mean is that it's okay to betray your boundaries.

I had a client, Mona, whose brother, Tim, drove around the Los Angeles freeways like he was on the Indianapolis 500 racetrack. Whenever Mona rode with him—to a Dodger game or a family day at the beach—she feared for her life. She put up with it, teeth clenched, for years, until the day he hit 85 on the 405 freeway. When they reached their destination, she calmly explained that she was not comfortable driving that fast. Tim laughed and said she was being ridiculous. Mona held her ground and asked if he would be willing to change his driving on the way home. He dismissed her request. She took an Uber home that night—and came to me to learn why she had allowed this relationship to devolve to that point.

As hard as it is to let go of a relationship, it is harder to stay in one where your need for basic boundaries is disrespected. "You don't ever have to feel guilty about removing toxic people from your life," says Daniell Koepke of the Internal Acceptance Movement. "It doesn't matter whether someone is a relative, romantic interest, employer, childhood friend, or a new acquaintance—you don't have to make room for people who cause you pain or make you feel small."[18]

Boundaries in everyday transactions

What about healthy boundaries in customer-provider relationships and other everyday transactions? If you feel intruded on, there are ways to politely set boundaries with strangers without being mean. When strangers get nosy, when they ask inappropriate questions, or when they touch you, get too close, or infer a level of intimacy that just doesn't exist, here are some phrases you might use to ask for what you want or to redirect the conversation:

- My preference is/I would prefer . . .
- I'd like it if/Is it possible to . . .
- I need . . .
- I can't make that decision right now.

Sometimes you might want to go even further. A manicurist once told me she was sorry I didn't have kids; I must be sad and lonely. Depending on our tolerance in such cases, we might use phrases such as these:

- I would like to talk to the manager.
- I would like to discontinue this conversation.

- I am not comfortable with this and am leaving.
- I would like another manicurist/clerk/waiter.
- I am not okay with this.

We can also simply vote with our feet and leave as soon as possible.

Setting safe boundaries with strangers

We teach kids about "stranger danger," and as adults we should also be wise and aware when dealing with people we don't know well, whether that is someone approaching on the street or someone we just met through a dating site. This is absolutely self-care. While many people we run into when out and about are lovely, there are some who simply aren't. I have taken to walking to my car with a determined stride, looking around and noticing who is near me. I also now keep my phone handy and my keys poised to serve as a weapon, if needed. I hate doing this, but the truth is that to do otherwise is self-neglect. Taking a self-defense class is as much a self-care strategy as having high-quality locks on one's home. And I have also reminded myself that I get to call the police if anyone touches me against my will.

Here are some good phrases to use when you feel your safety boundaries are being crossed by strangers:

- No! Stop! Back off!
- I don't want to discuss this with you.
- Do not touch me.
- This feels intrusive.
- I need you to give me some space.

Consider these safety strategies as part of your physical self-care repertoire, as well as part of your boundary-setting skill set.

Consider Saying No

Like boundary setting, saying no takes a strong sense of identity; it means taking responsibility for yourself, and it can offer immense relief. It is an answer that tells a questioner you aren't up for tacos, talking, taking the job, or getting a Peruvian parrot named Saul. And, like boundary setting, saying no is an act of self-care that is necessary for relationships. As writer Anne Lamott says, "No is a complete sentence."

When I first heard those words, it was a revolutionary thought for me, as a person prone to give excuses, caveats, or fifteen-minute explanations validating my truth. Even as I pondered it, I still had trouble saying no on its own, but when I started explaining my no, I at least understood that doing so was *optional.*

Today, saying no still takes effort, but Lamott's maxim is a comfort, and it allows me the freedom to know that I am entitled to my no. No doesn't mean that I don't love you, family member. No doesn't mean that I am "mean," coworker. I can say no to your request and still love you (respect you, care about you). No means you asked me a question and I chose an answer. No and love can and should go together.

One big reason we don't say no is that no isn't "nice"—or so we think. But is saying yes nice when we actually mean no? Is it nice to secretly suffer with resentment and bitterness, and do something that we don't want to do? Is lying and feigning the flu nice? We want people to like us, and so we do things in order to maintain the persona of nice. But if we say yes when we really want to say no to this thing, then we don't actually feel so nice; we feel like phony faker faces.

In the movie *Room,* based on Emma Donoghue's novel, a "nice" girl helps a stranger look for his dog (there is no dog), which leads her to being kidnapped and tortured for seven years. Finally, after her release, there's a not-so-nice moment when she tells her mother, "Maybe if your voice saying, 'Be *nice*' hadn't been in *my head,* then maybe I wouldn't have helped the guy with the fucking sick dog!" Self-care isn't being nice at the expense of yourself. *Room* is an extreme case, of course. But notice if nice is leading you into self-sacrifice, betrayal, and the opposite of self-care; if it is, then stop being nice. I give you permission.

If this is still hard for you, you might want to use a self-care rule that functioned like training wheels for me as I learned to recover from people pleasing. It's the "I need twenty-four hours to decide" policy. Following this rule prevents you from giving an automatic yes. It gives you time away from whoever has asked you to help them move, or to lend them a dress, or to travel to Chicago to give a speech, so you can figure out what you really want. (Remember principle 4: *Self-care means noticing what matters to us.*) This tactic has always served me well. No one has ever said, "You are a horrible person. How dare you take time? I hate you. Good-bye and good riddance." And if someone were to say that, then I imagine you know what the self-care response might be.

The opposite of saying no is asking for help

Learning to ask for what we want can be hard, for reasons we've already discussed. But we can't do this thing called life all alone, and so turning to people around us for tangible, emotional, and real support is an important element of self-care, and it's the exact opposite of saying no. In my own life, I have gone from thinking John Donne was wrong, and that I *am* an island, to having friends who have stepped up to help me in countless ways. Some traveled across the country to support me when I received a book award. One let me stay in her guesthouse when I was going through my divorce. In the wake of a neighborhood break-in, another offered to sit by my front door until I came home so my dog would be soothed by her presence. My ex helps me with my mother, who lives in a nursing home. My Facebook friends are always a post away from recommending a book, a movie, or a plumber. I have gone from having very little support to having an almost embarrassing wealth of support.

What changed? Not them, I can tell you; it was me. I am now willing to ask for help, to say, "I need you." Almost always, the benefit of asking for help is more wonderful than I could have imagined. And when help isn't forthcoming, that allows me to learn where to turn in order to get the help I need. Asking for help, like boundary setting, is a skill that can be learned and that gets easier in time.

Here's a tip: practice this skill during nonstressful times in your life, when the stakes are lower. When we are stressed, we're not in our most resourceful state. So think ahead: you might need help in a family crisis or other emergency, or you might simply need support during periods of stress.

I am so bad at asking for help that, when stressed, I tend to think that Bridget Jones's famous delivery of the anthem "All by Myself" is actually mine.

So, in the name of self-care, I've decided to tell a few key people up front what my rap is and out myself: *When I'm stressed, I may try to hide it, but here's what I'm likely to need.*

Two examples: My guy knows that when I've had a hard day, and I am so tired that I can barely speak, if he asks me what I need and I say, "Nothing," that means I likely need food, and I'd like him to say, "Oh, you poor baby." (No, I am not proud of this need for cooing, but I do crave it.) I have a lifelong friend who knows that when I've got a challenge coming up, I need to imagine the worst-case scenario and play that out, out loud, in order to know I'll survive no matter what. So we do that together.

Now ask yourself: *When I'm stressed, what am I likely to need?* And then, in advance, ask the people who love you for that: "I was wondering . . . when I'm stressed, would you be willing to _____?" (fill in the blank: hug me, encourage me, kiss my forehead). See how it goes. Some people won't agree to help, but that's useful information; it allows you to go ask someone else.

· · ·

Setting boundaries, saying no, and speaking your truth: these are all high-level Jedi Master self-care practices—what Oprah would do. Learning to set these boundaries and say no when you mean it benefits you, and it benefits your relationships. I know it is hard and scary, but you can do this!

And as hard as it is to say, "No, you can't use my garage to store your stuff," it might be harder still to face the way you are using stuff as a substitute for self-care. That's what we'll explore in the next chapter.

 If you look like a doormat, act like a doormat, and quack like a doormat, should you be shocked by the shoeprints on you?

SELF-QUIZ

Boundaries as Self-Care

1. In your family of origin, what were the rules about boundaries? How has that affected how you set or don't set boundaries?

2. Notice how you feel about *not* setting a boundary that you'd like to have. What have you feared would happen if you set it? What would happen if that outcome came to pass?

3. What do you think it will cost you to set boundaries? How do you know that is true?

4. What is the potential cost to your relationships when you don't make a boundary explicit? Lack of respect? Resentment? Hurt feelings? Divorce?

5. What boundaries do you need to set with friends, family, spouses, kids, co-workers, bosses? Why haven't you set these boundaries before?

6. What boundary phrases might you want to use with people who are close to you?

7. What boundary phrases might help you deal with strangers?

8. How okay are you with saying no? How can you use no as an act of self-care?

9. When have you said yes when you really wanted to say no?

CHAPTER NINE

Our Stuff, Ourselves

Self-Care and Our Belongings

The question of what you want to own is actually the question of how you want to live your life.

—Marie Kondo

WE TEND TO THINK OF OUR STUFF as our stuff and ourselves as ourselves. We think that one doesn't have much to do with the other, but that, my friends, is a big pile of Oscar Mayer bologna. Think of principle 4: *Self-care means noticing what matters to us.* Material things matter; those words come from the same root. Examining our possessions—and our attitudes toward them—can give us excellent insight into our values and our self-image. Remember, there's often more than meets the eye, but our belongings are an important form of self-care.

Our Stuff Is a Window to Our Soul

Okay, I know that isn't actually how the saying goes, but it's true. Every time we buy something, from a carton of milk to a cardigan to a car, we are engaged in a psychological action. Each action says something about our identity and how we would like to be treated, and it fulfills a psychological need. Every object we choose, buy, and possess—and even *how* we possess it and engage with it—sends a message to ourselves about the degree to which we matter or we don't matter.

We can't talk about self-care and ignore our stuff. (Or our money, which we'll discuss in chapter 10.) We have to live in our homes, with our stuff, and wear our clothes, and probably use a car. How we take care of this stuff, and how our stuff takes care of us, is all some serious psychological mojo and worthy of exploration. That's what this chapter is all about.

We'll start by looking through the lenses of White, Black, and Gray Magic self-care methods.

White Magic self-care and our stuff

Let's focus on home environments here. If I were to ask you what a self-care guru's house looked like, I'm guessing you might imagine a home that was sparkling clean with very well-organized shelves, lots of cozy corners for meditating, a wardrobe of the softest organic fibers in colors that align with our chakras, and a showroom-worthy car. No mess, no lost keys, no clutter, nothing tattered or torn. Everything mindfully chosen, sparkling with joy, humming with good feng shui.

Perhaps that's how some self-care experts keep their homes, but for most of us mortals, such perfection is unrealistic and not actually self-care at all. In some cases, this kind of environment might be the doing of a cruel super-ego that demands everything be perfect, even if achieving that perfection comes with a steep price—the peace and rest that's possible with "not perfect, but good enough." Self-care is not about being perfect: you've heard me strike that note before, and I will continue to hammer it like a highly polished Chinese gong. There is not just one way to engage in self-care. You may agree with that pristine White Magic ideal home environment, or you might have a different ideal. Either way, the ideal isn't the point. The point is finding what works for you—which we'll get to in a minute.

Black Magic self-care and our stuff

Stuff is nice, good, and even necessary. We all need pants and shoes, and maybe a car or a bike to get to work, and we need food and other supplies for survival. But the desire for maximum stuff (or minimum stuff) can also be destructive.

Let's look at a few of the Black Magic ways we can harm ourselves through our attitudes toward our belongings.

Compulsive buying can be seen as self-care run amok: consumption taken to a dangerous and pathological extreme. Experts on shopping addiction claim that people often overshop and overbuy to heighten their self-concept and mood, but the high of the buy is short-lived—hence the need to do it again and again. If you are after self-worth and belonging, stuff simply can't provide that in a meaningful way. So you don't get what you seek, and yet you still have to pay for it, often with hefty credit card fees and a plummeting credit rating. It's not a good trade.

Hoarding, like compulsive shopping, centers on stuff as a source of self-care, often giving it symbolic power. "Perhaps that's why I've never been able to throw anything away," says a character in Nicole Krauss's novel *The History of Love.*[19] "Perhaps that's why I hoarded the world: with the hope that when I died, the sum total of my things would suggest a life larger than the one I lived." Clinically, hoarding used to be considered an outgrowth of obsessive-compulsive disorder, but it is now seen as more related to anxiety, depression, and attention deficit disorder. People who hoard can't accurately assess the value of a given object; they keep everything because they can't determine what is or isn't necessary for their well-being. For many, hoarding is a way to deal with an underlying issue by creating a secondary issue that is more tolerable to the conscious mind. The core of the impulse is often a desire to feel safe and secure. Hoarders want to defend against loss and ensure all their needs are met—and yet, paradoxically, the more the person hoards, the more nontangible assets they're likely to lose. Eventually, functionality is lost, and safety, and the ability to move freely, to cook, clean, and sleep in their own home. Family and social relationships are strained and fractured. Again, it is not a good trade.

Masochistic minimalism: First, let's note that some of us live simple, minimalist, even ascetic lives, for all kinds of good reasons: spiritual, environmental, philosophical, social, political. Or we might simply lack financial means. But here I'm talking about a particular kind of minimalism: the withholding of stuff, comfort, and pleasure that is motivated by feeling unworthy. This kind of self-denial can cross the line into masochism. It may stem from early life; people who grew up with neglect, abuse, or trauma can struggle to feel they deserve anything good, telling themselves, "I didn't get my needs met then, so I am not going to have needs now." Whatever the reason, if you recognize this tendency in yourself, it can be important to start using stuff as a way to be kind, loving, and responsive to yourself. Giving yourself soft sheets, a clean home, and nutritious meals are small actions of moving toward a new way of treating yourself.

"The good stuff is for others": Although this may not be a true Black Magic practice, it's deeply harmful to us. If our sofa is covered with plastic and we have a vinyl walkway on the ivory rug, the message is clear: *We* don't deserve these good things; they're for *other* people. But the same self-denying instinct could manifest in less obvious ways; for example, you use the good china, towels, or wine only when you have company. Maybe you need guests before you'll finally use the dining room, buy flowers, or light candles. Maybe you use perfume only on vacation. Don't get me wrong: I know money doesn't grow on trees, and you can't splash out the Dom Pérignon every night—unless you can, and then bully for you. And yes, you might want to save that perfume for a special occasion, to heighten the experience. But let's make that a conscious decision. If it's not, you may be telling yourself that what matters most is how people perceive you. Is that a message you want to stick with?

Gray Magic self-care and our stuff

Even if we aren't compulsive shoppers or hoarders or masochists, we may, on occasion, dabble in some "quick-fix" stuff-related remedies that might qualify as Gray Magic self-care. We might buy, or hold on to, stuff as a means of changing our mood and self-concept, as a sort of substitute for higher-quality self-care. In using *things* to take care of deeper needs, we might overindulge in buying ourselves goods and goodies. Or we might hold on to items that serve as a proxy for love and self-worth (old teddy bears, dusty awards, love letters— even from people who hurt us).

This attempt at self-care says, "I am being unkind to myself in other areas of my life, so I am going to be extra good to myself via my stuff." It is the "I need a carrot to tolerate the stick" methodology. This kind of self-care can manifest in ways big and small, from impulse-buying lip balm to splurging on a Lamborghini. Whatever the item's size, you're using stuff to make up for not getting enough sleep, not having boundaries, ignoring your truths, or not having time to take care of your mind, body, and spirit. You're in a danger zone.

Often this kind of Gray Magic self-care comes along with the message *I deserve this.* I wouldn't dare say that you don't deserve a new eighty-inch television, but I might say it may not give you what you really need. If you are working eighty hours a week and the TV is a kind of emotional corrective for a lack of free time, it would be better to take a good hard look at the lack of balance in your life and instead give yourself what you really want that TV to give you. Stuff can be great, but there is a limit to what it can do.

When you find yourself shopping because you are tired, angry, hurt, or sad and you want to change your mood, just remember that you are seeing a "pony" (see chapter 5). The pony might give you a temporary escape from the feeling, but the feeling is going to be there even after the new-shoes high has worn off.

Whenever we shop, we're shopping for an underlying need or value— security, love, self-worth, for example. As a friend of mine put it, "I never really realized it before, but everything I buy is really for self-care. A nail is for building something I may need; a spade is for planting something that pleases me; a piece of art is something to give me pleasure for years on end, as would be a piece of jewelry. All of that is really a form of self-care."

When you find yourself really wanting to buy something that's truly optional, it can be very helpful to determine what you hope the thing will give you. Say you were sitting around minding your own business and all of a sudden a brand-new food processor popped into your mind. "I want that," you say. And before you know what hit you, you've ordered a $379.99 Cuisinart.

Now who am I to stand between you and your ability to slice, dice, julienne, and puree? That desire itself is fine, but I want to know where it came from. What the heck do you want this food processor to give you? Go on, ask yourself. Perhaps you want to make gazpacho. Maybe what that *really* means is that you want to feel like you did when you were in Spain and your rental apartment had a food processor you used to make gazpacho every night. Maybe buying a new food processor signifies that you want to entertain more and have the delightful feeling of creating your own tapenade and serving it to your grateful and gobbling guests. If so, what you really need is a bigger and more active social life. Is the Cuisinart going to give you that? I can tell you that I have one sitting in my appliance graveyard (cabinet), and it hasn't made me the least more social. That requires you to contact friends and have them over. But maybe the Cuisinart will be the lynchpin for you. The trick is to know what you *really* want and to buy things with the awareness that they're simply tools for achieving a deeper desire.

Sometimes knowing what you actually want from a thing will shut down the desire for the object. When you look closely, you might see that as much as you want to throw backyard soirees, the truth is that your schedule is crammed to the gills and that really, if being social is what you are after, there are better ways to go about it.

It's a fascinating exercise, uncovering these deeper needs. A young woman I know was craving cowboy boots, but when she really dug into it, she realized that she simply wanted to feel wilder and freer. A friend of mine who had suffered some recent deaths in his family paid a boatload of money for an analog 35mm camera. Why? He said he wanted to hold on to family memories and reclaim his high school days when he first learned photography and felt that he could do anything.

And several years ago I *really* wanted a trophy handbag. But before plunking down some serious cash, I decided to get clear about *why* I wanted this gorgeous Italian leather handbag with a luxurious red interior. The object was so beautiful that I had trouble allowing my ego to speak. But eventually things got clear. I realized that, upon surviving and thriving for one year after my divorce, I wanted a symbol to hold on to every day that reminded me of what I had achieved. The handbag became a totem for what I was capable of. And after becoming clear about why I wanted the bag, I still wanted the bag. Knowing gives you clarity, which gives you power.

Self-care signifiers in your life

There are likely things in your life—think of your closet or your car—that make you feel like you are taking care of yourself. For me, for example, all the items of my skin care collection are part of a major self-care habit. They are a bit indulgent in terms of cost and the time it takes to use them, but I feel cared about every time I apply my potions and lotions. I have a curated wardrobe that reflects my style and fashion philosophy, which goes a long way toward making me feel the way I want to feel in the world. I have a nearly anthropomorphic love of my bed pillows (one may have a name, and his name may be King Charles) and my blankets have to be super-super soft. I am not one for spending much time in the kitchen, but I do spend time every day with my Nespresso coffee machine. Is it a luxury? Yes, of course, but I am pretty picky about coffee, and using it makes me feel cared for.

Renee explains what some of her belongings signify to her: "I feel like I look after myself most in my bedroom and bathroom, where the bed is comfortable and there are lots of cushions, and I feel I can relax. My bathroom is kept relatively clean and full of soaps and cleansers to help us feel clean and comfortable as a family. There is a heated towel rail, so towels are usually clean and crisp to use, which is a comforting feeling."

Juanita, a writer who works from a home office, spends very little on her wardrobe or linens but lavishly on her writing tools. "I have a massive Thunderbolt screen, two desk lamps that deliver just the right kind of light, a paper calendar that has the precise design I love, and a ridiculously expensive chair that can be adjusted about a dozen different ways," she told me. "These tools remind me every day that what I am doing matters."

While we are easily able to identify items that contribute to our self-care, it can be a little harder to list how we use objects in ways that are *not* care inducing, such as

- habitually using our TV or computer to zone out
- keeping possessions that make us feel fat, ugly, poor, or that otherwise trigger our pain
- holding on to things that are broken, damaged, or possibly dangerous but that we refuse to fix
- purchasing luxury items as an attempt to be loved
- buying products we believe we need to feel "good enough"

Facing the way these items negatively affect our lives is an important part of self-care, too.

A word about mess and mayhem

I admit it, we'll never see a book titled *Keep a Messy House, Change Your Life.* But still, I believe that sometimes chaos at home can be a form of Gray self-care. Sometimes we are using mess to create a physical boundary—a way to prevent people from getting in. After all, if the living room is so messy you couldn't possibly invite anyone over, you don't have to worry about having anyone over. While obviously it's better to be clear about your need for boundaries, and about who you would really rather not see, I think that some mess and some imperfection in housekeeping is actually fine. Now, a certain man I live with might see this paragraph as self-serving, but I am okay with that.

Again, the past informs the present. I grew up in an extremely tidy household, not a relaxed environment. So for me it is self-caring to live in a home where it is acceptable to have a chair that holds all the clothes I wore yesterday. I will never let the clothes spill to the floor—there are limits. But to me, my willingness to allow my desk to look like a low-grade hurricane has hit is not at all disruptive or irritating. Sure, I would like to have an organizational fairy who would keep my bedside chair free of clothes and my desk beautifully spare, but such tidiness isn't a self-care necessity for me.

It's all about context. Remember principles 5 and 6: *Self-care requires attention and responsiveness* and *Self-care must be realistic to be effective.* For some, a house that's neat as a pin is self-care, while for others, an unmade bed and some dishes in the sink are indeed a way of saying, "There are other ways of taking care of myself than this, and I'm going to give myself a break."

Not only do I tolerate some messiness at home, but my decor shows that the stiff, formal home of my childhood is not where I want to be today. As a compensation, I now tend toward comfort (couches made for napping), sensuality (faux fur blankets, down-stuffed pillows), and a feeling of being relaxed and at ease. For me, it is much more important that a house feel livable than highly designed and perfect. Perfect, to me, would be the opposite of self-care. Perfect makes me want to break out in hives.

But if your childhood home was explosive and chaotic, never neat and calm, your self-care might involve creating a home that is über-organized.

That might involve having your spice rack alphabetized, your cabinets lined, and your shoes in Container Store boxes. Whatever you feel called to do in your home to care for yourself is what you should do.

Reviewing and Re-choosing Your Stuff: An Act of Self-Care

What would you do if your husband had the baseball game blaring at full blast in one room, your daughter was playing music down the hall, and your son and his pals were yelling in the rumpus room? *Something* is the answer; you would do something. Nobody could take that kind of noise.

But there's another kind of irritation, a "noise" we are all dealing with daily: to me, it sounds like a slow steady whine: *Waaaaaaah!* It's the low-grade but persistent whine of things, objects, that annoy us. Cheryl Richardson, author of *Take Time for Your Life*, calls them an energy drain: the broken or damaged things that remind you of something you need to do.[20] I get that. Every time I look at the dry cleaning sitting patiently on the bench, I see work. When I see those shoes that I need to take to the shoe guy, I feel a sense of burden and "Damn, I really need to do that." When I go to wear those pants that I haven't had hemmed, I hear that *Waaah!* The broken handle on the filing cabinet that distracts us, the cruddy shower curtain that sullies our shower experience—*I really need to replace that.* For most of us, we have lots of such small irritations that make little pinches on our energy, and self-care can mean dealing with them.

In not dealing with these things, the *Waaah!* gets louder, and the more of them there are, the greater the noise. We try to turn down the volume by telling ourselves, "I will deal with it later; I don't have time now." We never have time. But taking care of these kinds of tasks can really affect how you feel in your home. Can you imagine the joy of going into every room in your house without having to bat away the gnat of *I really need to get that fixed*?

And it's not just broken items. Try making a list of everything in your home that irks or dissatisfies you in some way. In compiling such a list, you might find that you hate the stupid fake orchid in your bathroom. Why on earth would you keep something you hate? Guilt is often a part of the reason, and fear of being wasteful, or not wanting to hurt Aunt Matilda's feelings if she gave you the stupid fake orchid. The truth is that you love Aunt Matilda and you hate the orchid. Get rid of the orchid!

On the other hand, I have a nativity scene made of Popsicle sticks that I would fight you Krav Maga style if you asked me to give up because it was made for me by a special woman I worked with at a retirement home. It is wonderful to have things that make you feel great. But if you're hanging on to items on the ugly orchid end of the spectrum, it may be time to remove those guilt-inducing objects from your environment. Making those choices is an important act of self-care.

Sparking joy?

Once you've figured out what items in your home bug you, you might be ready to decide what brings you joy. Marie Kondo, the Japanese organizational goddess and author of *The Life-Changing Magic of Tidying Up*, takes our relationship to our stuff to a whole new level. Kondo recommends that we go through *all* of our stuff, and I mean all of it, taking on full categories all at once—all of your clothes, your books, your papers, your sentimental stuff—and holding each item in your hot little hands to see if it "sparks joy." If it doesn't, then you give it the boot: donate it, pass it on, and let others enjoy it. In this process, you are keeping things based on what sparks joy and losing everything that doesn't.[21]

Caveat: some things that don't spark joy are still practical and useful. For example, I just don't care if my toaster sparks joy—it sparks bread into toast, so I'm keeping it. But I took on the task last year of touching all my stuff, Kondo-style, and while I am highly dubious about the concept of house spirits, I do think that bringing mindfulness to our relationships with our home, our stuff, and our wardrobe will help us in myriad ways. It feels very good and self-caring to be surrounded by things that I love, not by things I'm keeping because they were expensive, shoes that I love and would wear if they actually fit, or things that other people have told me I should keep (or like, or want).

I Kondo-ized my house in one week, which was a breakneck pace, and I can tell you that it was extremely difficult and emotional work. It felt like a psychological boot camp of awareness. It was hard to face all the ways I had settled, how much I was motivated by guilt and feelings of "I guess this is good enough" when it really and truly wasn't.

As I was going through my goods, touching and assessing (within reason) for joy, I saw how often my desire to keep something was based on guilt, cost, or fear. For example, when I was touching a particular pair of trousers to see if there was any joy in them, I remembered that they itch and scratch, and whenever I put them on I feel like I'm allergic to them. After identifying all of those Claritin-inducing reasons to part with these pants, I *still* felt like I should keep them! Why? *Well,* I thought, *they're a designer label I like. They were expensive. The color is gorgeous. They go with a lot.* But, um . . . excuse me, they itch, they scratch, and if I wore them in public people might think I have fleas. The expensive, beautiful designer pants needed to get out of my closet and into the donation bag. I mean, really? Keep them? Ridiculous. It is not a good use of my limited closet real estate to store pants that I will never wear and that *I only keep to avoid feeling bad about getting rid of them.*

The pants are now, I hope, the property of some woman who isn't as easily irritated by scratchy rayon. Better she has them and enjoys them than they sit in my closet unused, unworn, and unloved.

As hard as the pants were to part with, things got even more real when I dug into the sentimental stuff. It was awful to see all the pictures from my childhood that I kept around where I looked obviously sad and extremely lonely. It was an act of self-definition to say that all my philosophy texts and art books no longer sparked joy, and it was sort of sad to recognize that I was no longer that person who enjoyed such reading material. It took psychological heavy lifting to let go of relics from previous relationships. It was akin to bikini waxing when I made the bold, brave, and psychologically sound move to let go of the book filled with all the receipts, test records, and paperwork documenting my failed IVF cycles. As hard as it was, it was an extraordinary act of self-care to let all of this stuff go.

One of the benefits of Kondo-izing is that if you follow her theory to the letter, you will be left only with things you love and things that "spark joy." It has been over a year for me now, and I have fallen off the wagon when it comes to rolling my socks and T-shirts into beautiful origami Tootsie Rolls.

Nevertheless, I am still affected by the experience and believe that my home and my psyche have changed as a result. Now when I shop, before I impulsively put something into my cart, I ask myself if this item sparks joy. Do I really love it? Obviously, I don't do this when buying a honeydew melon (because clearly honeydew melon sparks joy) or when picking up a tube of toothpaste, but I do it with almost everything else. I now make fewer shopping mistakes, and fewer things end up in the giveaway bag with the ugly orchid.

More important, this exercise has had profound life consequences, even beyond my possessions. Because of the great Kondo clean of 2015, I am much more cautious and careful about what else I let into my life. I ask myself, *Does this project spark joy? Does this party spark joy? Does this book that my book club is choosing to read spark joy?* It went from being about *stuff* to being about my *life*.

· · ·

Like our stuff, our money can offer a lens into our priorities and our self-care habits. And that's the subject of the next chapter. We'll explore how we use money to care for ourselves and, conversely, how we use money to act out against ourselves. We'll discover that money care *is* self-care.

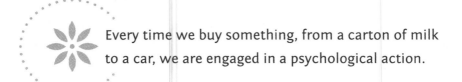

Every time we buy something, from a carton of milk to a car, we are engaged in a psychological action.

SELF-QUIZ

Self-Care and Your Stuff

1. Think about your possessions: home, clothing, technology, car or bike, whatever else is key in your material life. Which areas show great self-care, and which not so much? Do you keep your car shiny and neat but buy scratchy toilet paper? Why the discrepancies?

2. Think about your family of origin. How might your self-care with stuff be a compensation for the conditions you endured growing up?

3. In taking care of your stuff, how important is order, cleanliness, and comfort? What are your primary values connected to how you want to feel about possessions? Where do you think those values originate from?

4. Do you feel that your possessions communicate an attitude of self-love, self-neglect, or something in between?

5. Do you have possessions that make you feel especially taken care of?

6. Do you buy yourself objects as treats to make up for a lack of self-care in other areas? What are your treats? What are they making up for?

7. Are there things you hoard? What do they tend to be?

8. Do you save the good stuff for others, or for special occasions? Why?

9. What is your thought about deserving or not deserving? Is it okay for you to have stuff? Is it okay to take care of yourself through objects?

Money Care Is Self-Care

LET'S REVIEW: Self-care is not just for the rich and privileged. We busted that myth in chapter 1. Self-care is not about fancy smoke-free candles, massages, and spa getaways in exotic locales. Yes, those things are nice, but they are not necessary for self-care.

Self-care is an attitude of loving kindness, a way of talking to yourself, a way of considering your needs, and at the very core, it is about being an adult. Kids depend on others to care for them; adults take care of themselves. Of course, as adults we may depend on others to some degree. For example, we may depend on a spouse or significant other financially. But even if you're 100 percent dependent on someone else for your income, it's still up to you how you care for yourself in myriad ways. The boundaries you set don't cost money, and the way you talk to yourself is entirely free.

So before we get too far into the money talk, let me remind you of just a few major budget-friendly ways to boost your self-care: meditation, hugs, saying no when you mean no, going for walks, napping, journaling, unfriending people on social media who make you feel crappy, watching YouTube videos on money management, organic gardening, and Marie Kondo–style sock folding.

And let me add a disclaimer: I am not an MBA; I am an MFT, a marriage and family therapist. I am not giving you financial advice—that is outside of my scope of practice. I am talking self-care here. This chapter is not a financial guidebook; it's about viewing money as a self-care vehicle and shifting your attitude in how you engage with it. Start your motors!

Money and Mindfulness

As a therapist, I hear people talk about all kinds of things: loss, betrayal, heartbreak, humiliation, failures, deep insecurities, scandals, and secrets. You know what I don't hear much about? Sex and money. And if pressed, people would much rather talk about their favorite sexual position and hand over a list of their sex partners than talk about their money and their relationship to it. Yet the truth is that we all deal with this topic, whether we have a trust fund or no funds at all. Whatever your circumstances, understanding your relationship to money is absolutely necessary for your self-care.

Let's go back to our old pal Maslow and his hierarchy of needs. Right above our physiological needs are our security needs. We need certain things in place to feel safe, and financial security is one of them. We need money to take care of ourselves in even the most basic way. Rent. Food. Health care. These all take cash, so taking care of our money is taking care of *us*. I know that dealing with money is hard for many of us, but here, let's think about money as a mindfulness activity and not as an Excel spreadsheet of dread. Paying attention to your savings, insurance, debt, retirement accounts, disability policies, and budgets can be a loving declaration of caring for yourself without creating worry and anxiety. Instead of financial spreadsheets, I call them "How I mindfully and consciously choose to spend the money I created so I can be at peace" spreadsheets.

Let's think White Magic self-care for a moment. We all know what we *should* be doing financially; the ideal here is clear. We should be saving money. We should have a good credit score. We should spend responsibly. We should have retirement funds, 401(k)s, and medical, dental, and long-term care insurance. We shouldn't have debt. Knowing all these "shoulds" is easy—but the devil comes in the details. How *much* to save, how *much* to put into retirement, what *kind* of insurance policy? The *hows* of White Magic money self-care can be very confusing, so it's easy to say, "I'm just not going to do it." However, before you throw your checkbook across the room in despair, let's look at the psychological reasons we may be avoiding the White Magic and how we might be using Gray Magic instead.

What We Might Say to Avoid Dealing with Money

If we avoid dealing with money, our financial habits probably aren't in the Blinding White category. We may be managing okay financially, but we're somewhat passive and probably in some shade of Gray. Let's look at some common attitudes that keep us stuck there.

"Financially, I don't feel like an adult."

While doing research for this book, I queried a broad variety of people on social media about whether they feel like an adult around money. I was astounded by how many people said no—and many of them were well over the drinking age, had other little humans whom they were responsible for, and sometimes even had adult children of their own. What reasons did they give? Some examples:

- I don't make money decisions like an adult would.
- I don't make enough money/I don't have a real job.
- I haven't saved enough.
- I have debt/I don't have any debt.
- I don't own a house.
- I have bad credit/I had a bankruptcy.

Even if we don't *feel* like adults around money, the truth is that we *are* adults, and part of our self-care, as adults, is to take care of our financial lives. If we are using our money to avoid feeling like an adult—and hoping that someone else will take care of everything or that we will win the lottery or inherit the farm or marry a prince or princess—we are infantilizing ourselves.

We're also not using very good logic, because when people do win the lottery or inherit the farm, they have more complex money problems than they did before. And people who hand over the financial reins to someone else tend to be the sort of people whose bank accounts get wiped out by unscrupulous predators.

The truth is that you are an adult and you already *are* taking care of yourself financially. I am just asking you to no longer do the standard "good-enough" self-care with money. I am asking you to upgrade your relationship to conscious financial self-care, from Medium Gray to a maybe a Light Dove Gray.

Instead of hoping to marry someone who is rich, why not instead, in the spirit of self-care, start dating yourself financially. Get to know your money life slowly; you don't want to go all the way and do major lifetime financial planning on the first date, so start slow. Bari Tessler, financial therapist and author, suggests money dates.[22] You know, light a candle, decant some Pellegrino into a fancy-pants cup, play some music that puts you in the mood to get intimate with your finances, and start slow—slow is key. Maybe you start with looking at how much money you are making and what your credit card bills are. Then, on the second date, you research a way to track income and expenses, such as with Mint or QuickBooks. When you're getting closer to your finances, and maybe even have a pet name for your financial relationship, like Pooky or Mr. Big, perhaps it is time to look at your credit score and then make a plan for how to improve it by getting a referral to an accountant.

You might decide to make a weekly date with your finances and show up for it without fail: that's what author Kate Northrup suggests in *Money: A Love Story.* This is, after all, a relationship. And what happens when you don't show up for your relationship and you ignore it? You get left for someone who does show up. Pay attention, and the relationship gets better. Imagine a couple walking on a beach at sunset: you and a big dollar bill. Think of you and your money as a love story.

Are you resisting? Take it even slower. Start where you are. Use these ideas for those early money dates.

- Check in with your body and try to identify what exactly you are feeling. Your resistance probably has something important to share with you.

- Scan the scenery of your money relationship. Ask, "What is my next baby step?" Clean your basement files? De-clutter the emails from your bank? Unpack a painful money story? Remember to start slow.

- Zoom out for some perspective: What season of your life are you in? What are your money goals? Sometimes we need to step outside of our "money to-do's" and use those early dates to shed light on the bigger picture.

- Use a date to feel grateful for the wealth, abundance, and resources you *have* created for yourself—even if your bank balances are not where you want them to be.

Still, you might say to me, "I don't want to deal with my money because I will feel inadequate, and *not* dealing with money feels like self-care to me, so stop pushing this topic, Tracey. I liked your book up to this point, but now I'm sort of over you."

I hear you. Avoiding something in order to feel good can look like Gray self-care, but it doesn't work. Putting your hands over your ears and singing "La-la-la-la, I can't hear you" isn't going to work. What do you imagine are the consequences of this mind-set? I will tell you: you will feel bad today when you wallow in denial because it is denial with a capital D, and you will feel worse tomorrow when you have late fees, high interest, low credit scores, bounced checks, and nothing in the bank to sail off into the sunset in your golden years.

Be gentle with yourself. This need not be a financial root canal. Each time you sit down face-to-face with your finances, breathe deeply and remind yourself that you are enough. All you are doing, after all, is bringing consciousness to this important area of your life.

"I'm not good at this stuff."

In telling yourself, "I am not good at this stuff," you are trying to let yourself off the hook. Truth be told, maybe you *aren't* good at this stuff. Okay, that's fair, but you can learn. You didn't used to be so good at speaking, walking, or going to the bathroom in the proper place—you learned those skills, right? Dealing with finances is a skill that can also be learned. Break it down. Ask yourself, *What exactly I am not good at? What do I need to learn? How can I learn it? Do I need a financial advisor? A wealth advisor? An accountant? Books? A class? Podcasts?*

As a first-time small-business owner, I was not good at all kinds of things. I was scared to get help, so I made a point of finding a kind and compassionate accountant. Her voice is soothing to me—she has the kind of cooing tone that would be perfect for reading aloud at the children's library. I feel like she is taking care of me. I always notice she has a box of Kleenex on her desk and something about its presence has given me permission to cry if I need to. I haven't needed to, but it is a comfort to know the Kleenex is there.

Each time I saw her in the beginning, I worried that she would judge me. I felt ashamed. I could have let this fear stop me, or I could do what I learned to do: breathe through the fear and remind myself over and over that the reality of the situation doesn't match my fears. This accountant is kind, helpful, and a financial superhero who doesn't expect me to know everything. Let me reiterate this truth: *wealth-building professionals don't expect us to know everything.* They don't judge us—just as therapists don't judge us for having issues, doctors don't judge us for being sick, and teachers don't judge us for entering their class for the first time and not having mastery of their subject. It is okay to get help. We don't have to know it all. Financial awareness and money management skills are things we can learn.

"I'll never have enough money, so I'd rather not think about it."
I know this one. I hate that "I don't have enough" feeling. No one likes it. It taps hard on other "I am not enough" feelings. But a bank balance does not get to determine who you are. No number defines you, whether it be your weight, your size, your grade point average, or your bank balance. Yes, the number may affect how much you can spend or what bills can be paid, but it is not a self-defining number.

When you look at your finances, you need to determine what amount is enough for you to have the life you want. When you know this number, you can make modifications to your spending or your work life to make it a reality. Budgeting might help with that process—see below if budgeting scares the crap out of you.

When we identify the truth of what we want, then we can make decisions consciously to meet our financial goals and modify our saving, spending, working, and investing to get to "enough." If we don't get clear about what enough is, we might never feel like we have enough or are enough, and that is a feeling that is most definitely not about money.

"Not now—I have some important purchases coming up."

I am familiar with the Varuca Salt form of financial planning. You remember young Varuca, who famously had a major tantrum at Willy Wonka's chocolate factory: *"I want it all and I want it now!"* This is most certainly an attempt at Gray financial self-care. This mind-set often correlates with not being an adult when it comes to money and amassing over-the-top credit card debt.

The truth is that delayed gratification is part of mature money management. I get it: you want something and you want it now. You feel you deserve it, and you likely do. I know that you deserve a handmade Swiss watch with platinum and gold casing or a sparkly new car, but that deserving may not at present match your bank balance.

As we discussed in chapter 9, often what we want is a stand-in for something else. When we want the gorgeous watch, what we *really* want is a symbol of success, or a "treat" to make some drudgery seem worthwhile, or a way in our social group to feel a little more alpha, less omega. But let's take time to understand what our inner Varuca wants before we click the trigger on that online shopping cart. What do you *really* want? Will this give it to you? Does this purchase support your financial goals? Notice how your body feels when you ask these questions. Yes, it would feel good now to buy it. But how would it feel next month to see it on your credit card bill? Again, I am not trying to stop Varuca from getting what she wants—perhaps just from getting it *right now*. Delayed gratification can be a high-level self-care activity.

And it doesn't mean that you can *never* have that thing you want. If you really want that Airstream trailer and you can't afford it now, crunch the numbers to find a way to make it happen. What changes in your work or spending life would put you in that Airstream in a year, two years, five years? Are you willing to do what is necessary in order to afford that item?

"Money management means budgets, and budgets cramp my style."

Not budgeting may feel like self-care. But it's dangerous Gray Magic that can lead to a hot mess so significant that soon you're feeling the Black Magic of massive debt and bankruptcy. Budgeting is a major act of financial self-care. And yet for some folks the very word *budget* feels constricting, ensuring that they'll never get to do "anything fun again, ever!"—which gives you a clue that a tantrum is happening. Budget is not a four-letter word. It won't take away your fun stuff or your freedom; it will actually let you save for what is really important to you.

Before I met Keith, I had never done a budget. When Keith suggested we do one together, I let out a *"But I don't want to"* whine that sounded like the three-year-old version of myself, which is not attractive in a middle-aged professional. So I relented, or should I say that I reluctantly endured the hell of watching him plop numbers into Excel boxes. And as hellacious as it was to sit for thirty minutes as my income and expenses were set out before me, it turned out to be a liberating experience.

Keith loves budgets, Excel, and QuickBooks, and for that I feel extraordinarily grateful. And now I'm changing my ideas on budgets and turning them into something a little more self-care-friendly to my non-mathematical mind.

This budgeting makeover started with red velvet cheesecake at the Cheesecake Factory. Let me explain: I have, on a few occasions, indulged in a piece of this delicious and highly satisfying cheesecake—that is, before I started to track my food in my fitness app. When I did, I was astonished to discover that a single slice of this cheesecake had 1,250 calories. 1,250? That is a *whole lot* of cream cheese. As soon as I saw the caloric cost, this cheesecake dropped from my "maybe occasionally" list to my "no way, ever" list. Willpower wasn't necessary. I simply didn't want it anymore. You, on the other hand, might say, "Yes, I absolutely want to budget in for a weekly cheesecake," and that's great; there's no right or wrong here. But if you want the cheesecake and you also don't want to gain weight, then you need to figure out where you might be willing to modify your intake in other places.

Now hold on to your red velvet, because I believe that the same trick can work for finances. If you actually take a look to see how much you spend each year on dining out, cable TV, and your two-Starbucks-a-day habit, it might inspire a change. You would either decide that "yes, I absolutely feel that cable TV is worth $2,500 a year" or you would quickly call your cable provider (and then promptly sit on hold for the next forty-five minutes) to cancel your service. Awareness can lead to change. You either choose to keep things the way they are (without the denial and guilt), or you choose to change. Either way, you are no longer acting unconsciously.

When I did this exercise, I got to see how much my mindless one-click Amazon.com orders were costing me in a year. When that number turned out to be higher than what I paid for my second car, I immediately developed a mindfulness practice on Amazon.

Another number I didn't love was in the restaurant category. For two adults who aren't big winers and diners, it was a bit shocking. But it's an expense that makes our lives easier and more fun, and dining out is how we break out of work mode. The awareness made me look and see that I actually really value going out to dinner. In this case, the awareness didn't create change; it just made me realize how much I actually enjoy what we are doing. It heightened my appreciation and made me aware that eating out gives us a lot of value (time alone, beautiful environments, a feeling of occasion, "off-duty" time for both of us, and delicious food).

Looking at how you are currently spending your money will not only help you track where it's going; it will help you reassess what you actually value and where you want to spend your hard-earned cash in the future.

When Green Turns Black: Avoiding the Worst-Case Scenarios

For those in the mental health field, the *Diagnostic and Statistical Manual of Mental Disorders* serves as a key reference book, describing these disorders and their symptoms in great detail. The current (fifth) edition of this manual is known as *DSM-5*. I find it interesting that the *DSM-5* includes very little about disorders related to money and self-care, or lack of it (although gambling addiction is described). And yet, in my experience, money problems are often a part of what people talk about when they come in for therapy on everything from depression to divorce.

As we noted in chapter 9, compulsive shopping holds extreme danger for our well-being, as the shopper tends to continually seek the next buying high—which won't last long, either. Let's just note here that compulsive shopping is also super-dangerous for our financial well-being. Even if the shopper starts with plenty of green, these Black Magic self-care attempts can bring it low pretty fast. In the worst-case Black Magic scenario, people try to make themselves feel better by buying the too-big house, and the boat, and the pony and all of the stuff that goes with it, ignoring reality to such a degree that they lose everything and must declare bankruptcy.

If this is where you are—or where you are heading—then it is time to get some help, and not just legal and financial. It is time to look into how you got into this situation and what you are trying to give yourself through this experience. One wonderful resource is Debtors Anonymous, a support community for people struggling with compulsive overspending, debt, and financial impulsivity.

But other problems can lead to bankruptcy, too. Amid a medical crisis, unemployment, and other serious problems, declaring bankruptcy could actually be a wise and self-caring thing to do. Get good financial and legal help to aid in making that decision.

Upgrade Your Financial Self-Care

As noted above, I am not a financial expert, but I do have some advice for how to bring self-care into your financial life—and I have seen it transform people's relationship to money. Let's look at six ways to improve your own money self-care.

Reframe your bill paying through a new-agey lens

Paying bills is not anybody's hobby of choice. But what if you reframed the activity to be a celebration of all the awesome stuff you've already got? Perhaps you could think of each bill as a "Document of Where I Am Consciously Choosing to Put My Resources" and organize your bills as a gratitude/value practice. When I write the check each month for my home, I say: "I am writing a check for a home that I chose and that I love. My home gives me a sense of peace, freedom, comfort, and beauty, and I love it." Try it with your own monthly home payment. I know, it feels like a lot, and you might rather use the money to go to Hawaii, but if you make that payment consciously and elevate the activity to one that clarifies what benefits you get from your home, then your attitude may change, whether you're writing a check, clicking a button, or noticing the auto-payment in your account. Every payment, even a parking ticket, can be reframed: "This payment helps maintain the beauty, order, and infrastructure of a city I love. I choose to learn from this ticket, and I want to be more conscious about my time so I can choose to spend my money in another way."

Tiny splurges could help you avoid big splurges

I love and admire Suze Orman. Her perspective is often aligned with White Magic self-care, and if I listened to her absolutely, my bank balance would be a whole lot higher. But there are times when Starbucks makes a whole lot of sense from a self-care standard, albeit not so much from a budgetary standard. Yes, technically, it is always better to eat kale rather than salted caramel lattes. But if we're so rigid that we *never* get that salted caramel latte, we're more likely to oversplurge on something else that is probably worse. Without some quota of metaphorical lattes, life is going to feel hard, punishing, unrewarding. All savings and no splurge makes Jackie a dull girl.

Debt does not mean you are a bad person

I know *debt* is a dirty word, and you may choose to pay yours off ASAP. But there are times when debt is a great investment and perhaps the best thing you can do for yourself. Even if you have a lot of debt, make it a learning experience. Write up a story describing what that debt gave you. For example, "Dear Self, I feel super crappy and ashamed about this debt, but let's look at what I really wanted from it and let's get to a place of understanding, insight, and compassion so that we don't continue to hold shame." Basically, what I am asking you to do is to learn from your debt, celebrate what it allowed for you, and then move on from it. Keeping debt in the dark makes it shameful. Spin that shame around, and bring light and insight to your debt.

I talked with a busy hospital nurse named Tonya about this subject. She reflected on some of the debt she'd incurred: "When I looked at where I was spending my money and what I wanted from it, I see that a lot of it came from feeling like I needed trips, treats, and trinkets to make up for all the stress I experienced at the hospital. Yes, I hate that it led to a $50K credit card debt, but now I have compassion for myself when I see that balance and am much more conscious about how I use my credit going forward."

Diane's debt is mostly related to her divorce. "While I wish that I didn't have it, I see that my debt allowed me to get out of a bad marriage," she told me. "And in order to feel safe, I needed a new car and to live in a secure build-ing. I was starting all over again, so I felt like I deserved everything in the Williams-Sonoma catalog. But looking at what I was really trying to achieve with my spending—to feel safe and secure and to have a home that felt like it was all mine and new—I get it. I understand the debt and I have compassion for it, and I no longer have the shame about it that it I once did."

Save for self-care emergencies

I'm not talking about a real financial emergency: that's a separate calculation (I save 10 percent of my income as a kit for life's bigger emergencies). But my self-care emergency kit contains $200. I keep that wad of self-care cash stashed in the back of a shelf. It is there for things like massages, new paja-mas, or a little luxury when I am feeling depleted. I recommend this idea for anyone, although how much you choose to save is very personal. What is universal is that both kinds of saving funds—serious emergency and self-care emergency—are necessary. And remember that as you set budgets, make sav-ing plans, and decide what you value, your self-care needs change. Remember principle 5: *Self-care requires attention and responsiveness.*

Cultivate gratitude for what you have and what you make

You and Donna Summer both work hard for your money (and if you are under thirty-five, feel free to google Donna Summer). Whether that money comes through a job, an unemployment check, a partner, or a trust fund, I strongly suggest you celebrate your current state. Every time you get a check in your hot little hand is an opportunity to celebrate what you have managed to create for yourself. You may say, "But I want more. I deserve more." Okay, fine. But do you think you are going to motivate yourself to take the steps necessary to achieve that if you keep putting down your ability to care for wonderful you? I think not.

Can you imagine a darling little first-grader showing you their report card and you saying: "Um, excuse me, that isn't a college degree, and I refuse to cel-ebrate you until you have a PhD"? No. Celebrate now. Celebrate every check. Honor the abundance you have created for yourself. Celebrate your ability to care for you. Hats and confetti optional.

See self-care as a way to be more prosperous

I have heard many self-help gurus, and even some psychotherapists I know, claim that taking care of yourself and seeing yourself as deserving good affects how others treat you, what kinds of people you attract, and even the perceived value of the work or services you perform. Some folks believe energy is behind this increase in finances, and I suppose on some level I would agree with that. If we communicate to ourselves and others that we are worthwhile, that message gets out to folks, and conversely, if we feel we are undeserving and not worth taking care of, that also gets communicated to others.

I am not sure that self-care will make you any richer financially. I would like to believe that it does, but I am certain that incorporating self-care into our lives makes us feel more abundant, even if we haven't changed our financial situation. I know I feel more abundant when my mornings aren't so hectic, when I have the time to sit outside in my backyard and sip a cup of coffee with a friend. My perception of myself in that state feels more abundant even though my finances haven't changed one iota.

• • •

Let's close with an example. Alijah is a friend who shifted how she spends her food budget. Instead of buying the same old prepared foods she used to rush to eat at night, she's been stopping at a farmers market after work, buying fresh bread and cheese and tomatoes and peaches, and making each meal into a little celebration. She feels like she is living super large, but all she did was shift what kinds of food she eats and where it comes from. With this change, she feels more taken care of and nurtured in body and spirit, as well as part of a community. She feels more abundant, even though at the end of the day she is spending more or less the same as she was before.

That's the kind of shift you can make in your own financial life so that you, too, can feel richer every day.

 Imagine a couple walking on a beach at sunset: you and a big dollar bill. Think of you and your money as a love story.

SELF-QUIZ

Self-Care and Money Care

1. Do you use money to take care of yourself emotionally? How?

2. How do you go about financially taking care of yourself (in practical terms such as savings and insurance)?

3. Do you feel like an adult around money? If not, how do you feel?

4. What financial decisions do you make that aren't very self-caring?

5. Is it okay in your worldview to want money?

6. Which—saving or spending—feels more like self-care to you? Is there a balance between the two in your life?

7. What were your family's beliefs about money, and how have they affected your ability to take care of yourself?

8. Do you have a budget? If not, how does that affect your feelings of being taken care of or provided for?

9. How do money and self-worth intersect for you?

10. What purchases do you make that feel like self-care to you—splurging on a trip, a personal trainer, or just a Frappuccino—no matter what Suze Orman might say?

CHAPTER ELEVEN

Self-Care at Work and Play

Work consists of whatever a body is obliged to do.
Play consists of whatever a body is not obliged to do.

—Mark Twain

WE MAY THINK THAT WORK is work and play is play, and that neither work nor play are domains that call for self-care. If that is what you think, I would say you (and the old me who believed the exact same things) are wrong. We can't restrict self-care to after-work hours and expect to do an adequate job of it (forty to eighty hours a week of ignoring self-care is a whole lot of ignoring). What's more, ;how we play or don't play is very much a part of our self-care plan. Maybe your thinking and actions are similar to what I used to do. I used to believe that work was my self-care (achievement, success, and creating security for myself) and that play was stupid and something only for the two weeks of vacation where I practically collapsed on a beach chair out of exhaustion. Both of us can do better than that; I know we can!

Self-Care at Work

Work may seem like the opposite of self-care. It may seem more like a time of self-sacrifice or self-denial. But let's think about exactly why you work. What is it you're trying to get out of work? Could it possibly be to take care of yourself? To find personal satisfaction and meaning, and to earn the money you need to put a roof over your head and shoes on your feet? Bingo! Yes, exactly!

Sometimes we forget that self-care is one of the main reasons we work. But, paradoxically, when we work we often completely quit caring for ourselves, thereby undermining the main benefit. In this chapter, we will put self-care back into your work life by looking at limits and boundaries, and making sure to find a way you can keep work meaningful and rewarding.

White Magic self-care at work

We can all guess what perfect self-care in work might look like: meaningful, productive, and financially rewarding work that also allows us time and energy for family, hobbies, and self-care in other areas of our lives. It's the elusive work-life balance—a balance that very, very few of us have. Let's talk about why this is the reality.

You might be familiar with the idea of the Protestant work ethic, whether you've taken an economics class or not. It's the philosophy that has so many of us feeling that work achievement and financial success should come before almost everything else in our lives. This idea was captured over a century ago by Max Weber, a German scholar and political economist. Through Weber, the Protestant theology of John Calvin and Martin Luther created a shift in Christian theology that would have far-reaching effects. In this worldview, the fruits of our relationship with God would be demonstrated and rewarded not just in the afterlife but here on earth. If you worked hard and succeeded, it meant that God had seen your efforts and would reward you with financial success.

Weber's legacy helps explain why people who live in the United States work more hours and take fewer vacations than people in other countries; on perhaps an unconscious level, we believe that all our hard work means we are good and virtuous. To do otherwise—to set limits, turn off our phones, and take an entire Sunday off, or, gasp, an entire week—is to be *not* so virtuous and to risk feeling like we are failing both morally and financially. We might even fear feeling less loved by God.

But the simple truth is that we don't become financially richer or more "successful" by going for a run on our lunch hour, taking vacations, or leaving the office with enough time to go to our kid's baseball game.

This is why, when it comes to work, Black Magic self-care sits so close to White Magic self-care. Let's flip over to look at the dark side.

Gray to Black Magic self-care at work

Workaholism may be the primary Black Magic self-care habit in this domain. In a recent study in Norway, researchers reported that 7.8 percent of Norwegians are workaholics. According to the *Harvard Business Review*, "The scientists cite a definition of workaholism as 'being overly concerned about work, driven by an uncontrollable work motivation, and investing so much time and effort to work that it impairs other important life areas.'"[23] By this definition, a lot of us in this country meet this Black Magic level of self-care in our work.

A forty-hour workweek? Ha! In the United States, most of us are clocking more like fifty or sixty hours, eighty for some of us. Living in a time with constant Internet access and smartphones that enable us to be available literally all the time, we may feel like we are never *not* working. And don't even get me started on stay-at-home mothers or working mothers—when exactly do they have time off? Never? That is totally unsustainable, and I am not sure why more people aren't losing their minds on this kind of schedule.

As in other areas of life, Black Magic self-care through workaholism is a healthy impulse gone astray; we are trying to take care of ourselves and our families and meet goals, which is all well and good. But when work goes into the territory where it is costing us health, damaging relationships, and preventing other primary self-care needs from getting met, then it turns into a toxic situation.

This is an area I know a whole lot about. My interest in self-care grew out of my work life. As I said before, we therapists are reminded all the time to do self-care because self-care prevents burnout, reduces compassion fatigue, and helps us do our best work, but no one ever teaches us what it means or how to do it.

Meanwhile, I was driving myself relentlessly. Seeing clients all day, skipping lunch and bathroom breaks, scheduling meetings after hours. So why did I work like this? Lots of reasons. I love what I do—I am passionate about it. Doing what I do makes me feel great, energized, and productive. But another part of me feels like it's my profession that makes me worthwhile and valuable. That is the me who, when people ask, "Tracey, how are you?" answers "Busy!" as if it were a badge of honor. If I am busy, I am successful and important. There is an element of masochism in being so busy that I ignore my basic needs. But remember what our friend Maslow said? You can't self-actualize if you aren't taking care of basic needs. "Burning the candle at both ends" is not a model for health and well-being. Instead, it turns us into self-sacrificing, red-eyed, antacid-eating labor zombies.

Principle 7: *Self-care precedes self-fulfillment.* I am happy to report that I am much better now that I've prioritized my own well-being—and I have more to offer my clients, too. But I still have days when I complain to Keith about how busy I am and how hectic my schedule is; he tells me I should fire my scheduler. Of course, I create my own schedule. (Physician, heal thyself!) Not everyone has the luxury of organizing their work life—bosses, spouses, and kids may call a lot of the shots. Even so, you can respond to the realities of your schedule and still find ways to let some self-care into your life.

NEEDLESSLY OVERWORKED: A CASE IN POINT

Are you the tiniest bit concerned that adding self-care into your daily life will make you less productive and successful? Not only is taking care of ourselves important for us as humans, it can actually make us more productive, effective, and creative workers. In their book *Well-being,* Ivan Robertson and Cary Cooper note, "Research has shown that people with higher levels of activity (such as exercise, creative activities, or social activities) appear to cope more effectively with the strain of work and recover better from work-induced fatigue."[24]

Let me reintroduce you to Keith, an extremely handsome, charming, funny, and successful sales guy (I may be talking him up because he is my fiancé). Before meeting me, Keith had what some might describe as workaholic tendencies. He brought those tendencies into our relationship, and since I am, shall we say, a somewhat driven person, I sort of liked his drive. Keith had a death grip on his phone most of the time, so he could immediately respond to customer texts, phone calls, and emails. This phone went to dinner, to the movies, to pedicures, to sleep, even on vacation with us. His outgoing phone message, "Leave a message and I will call you back right away," drove me bonkers. Well, after a relationship crisis, Keith realized that all the work and all the phone time was hurting him, his health, and his relationships.

And he changed. Now Keith never looks at his phone when we go out. It stays in the car when we go to dinner. He ends his day at 7 p.m. unless I am working late, and even on those days he still makes a point of stopping whatever he is doing when I come home to check in before finishing his task.

What's more, since Keith has made these changes, his sales figures have gone through the roof. When I asked him what he attributed the increase to, he said, "I think because I am taking time for myself and my health and my relationships that I have more energy and am actually more present for my clients. That shift in my energy from grinding and appearing overeager has had an incredible impact on how my clients perceive me, and that perception has led to an increase in sales."

I would make the argument that Keith was attempting to do self-care through his workaholic ways. There is so much social cachet, praise, and cash prizes that can come from being a workaholic, and he was trying to create feelings of security and control while "taking care" of himself and his family. Yet he was depleting himself and ignoring his real needs. Work is a slippery slope that way. You need to analyze how you are using work for self-care: is it a way to have time away from your family and time for yourself? A way to distance yourself from relationships that are working? Try to determine what secondary needs get met though your work, and then see if there is a way to get those needs met more directly instead of on the job.

Practical habits for self-care at work

You can bring self-care into your work in numerous ways. Try these; they can have powerful effects.

MANAGE YOUR TIME MINDFULLY

As you did with your finances in the last chapter, take a really honest look at how much you are working. Whether you are an eighty-hour-a-week surgeon or a 168-hour-a-week mother, you need to see what work is demanding of you and whether there is a way to bring self-care into your work life. Maybe the reality is that your work life won't allow you to take a day off just now. Still, try to sneak in some self-care. Avoid scheduling meetings with that difficult person first thing on Monday morning. And don't arrange to do the most difficult work of the day at 3 p.m., just as you start to lose energy. If you really feel stuck, perhaps it is time to talk to trusted friends, your mentor, a business coach, or a therapist to figure out a way forward. Look for micro-changes you could make to your work schedule that can make it more pleasant and more aligned with self-care.

You can learn actual time management tricks in books such as *The 4-Hour Workweek* by Timothy Ferriss, *Getting Things Done* by David Allen, and *Deep Work* by Cal Newport. But I want to talk here about time management as self-care.

Time management from a self-care perspective might look like this:

1. Not loading any one day with too many stressful activities.

2. Scheduling activities that matter to you other than work, so they are there on the calendar and can't be bumped off so easily. This might include workouts, tea with friends, or time to browse in the local library. Whatever it is, write it in ink.

3. Avoiding multitasking. Multitasking is as elegant and effective as patting your head and rubbing your stomach at the same time. Earl Miller, a neuroscientist and professor at MIT, says that our brains really can't do two things at once: "Switching from task to task, you think you're actually paying attention to everything around you at the same time. But you're actually not."[25]

4. Creating a list of top priorities for the day and doing those first. Having those biggies behind you will make you feel accomplished, relieved, and less likely to have that hair-on-fire feeling.

5. Setting boundaries around availability. There are times when we need to *not* be available to co-workers, employees, bosses, and even friends and family.

6. Resisting the temptation to overbook. Don't say yes to something before you take a look at your schedule; even though a dinner out with friends sounds lovely, it won't be lovely if you're so overtired that

you are incoherent and drooling. And don't, if at all possible, accept new work responsibilities without considering if you have the self-care resources necessary to take on the task.

RESIST THE "ALWAYS-ON" MENTALITY

I don't know how many times I have had conversations with people about the curse and blessing of technology that allows us to be available all the time. I am old enough to remember a time before answering machines, and back then if you were out, it was too bad—the person would call you later. Now there is no uninterruptible space or time. Thanks to technology, we can always be working.

Many people use this constant connectivity and the demands of "but I got a text for work" as a substitute for self-care. Checking for "likes" or to see if you got a pellet of approval in the form of some praise or a new order can become distracting—and addicting. Take a hard look at how much you are using your phone, iPad, and computer as a form of Gray Magic self-care.

In the ever-changing landscape of apps, you'll find tools to bring your tech use out of your unconscious and into awareness. In her book *The Future of Happiness*, Amy Blankson suggests downloading the Instant or Moment apps—which are kind of like Fitbits for your phone, only here the higher the number, the more likely you are in Gray Magic territory. Just being aware of how much time you are spending—or wasting—on your phone may help you clean up the habit a little. You'll free up time to incorporate other methods of self-care, like taking real breaks instead of social media breaks.

It also helps to be aware of *why* you are reaching for the technology. When I have the sudden impulse to reach for my phone and search my Instagram, I ask myself, *what do I want?* Do I want a break? There may be a more satisfying break. Am I bored? Am I tired? A nap might work better. Sometimes I *do* just want to see pictures of Westies, and then I let myself have at it. But checking in on what I really want and seeing if there is a better way to get it helps me be clear about my use of technology.

One fantastic trick for self-care around email is to choose not to do it first thing in the morning or last thing at night. Ideally we want to create an "electronic sunset" for ourselves; because of how these electronics affect our circadian rhythms, turning all screens off at least one hour before bedtime will help us fall asleep more quickly, let us sleep longer, and improve the quality of our sleep.

No matter your awareness of your tech dependency or your habits, it is imperative to occasionally have a block of time where *nothing* is demanded of you. Create tech-free times in the name of self-care, or just in order to be more efficient. You can turn your phone to airplane mode or use an app like Offtime or Unplugged if you need assistance with this.

TAKE BREAKS

We have all probably seen the amazing work environment that is Googleplex: a workplace utopian paradise of self-care. It features basketball courts, gyms, putting greens, massage rooms, and places to nap. If you work at Google, then you don't need to read this bit, but otherwise keep reading: Google doesn't do all of this because they are being nice. They do it because they know that people are more productive when they have breaks. According to K. Anders Ericsson, professor of psychology at Florida State University, we humans can't keep grinding nonstop without consequences. Dr. Ericsson looked at people in a variety of fields and found that in order for them to be the most successful, they can work no longer than ninety minutes at a time before taking a break. "Our bodies regularly tell us to take a break, but we often override these signals and instead stoke ourselves up with caffeine, sugar and our own emergency reserves—the stress hormones adrenaline, noradrenaline and cortisol."[26] If you aren't working in an environment where you can step into a spontaneous game of hoops, there are other ways to respond to the ninety-minute productivity cycle.

Here are ten self-care activities you can do on a ten-minute break:

1. Take a walk or do some stretches.

2. Close your eyes. If you don't have a private office, perhaps your car could suffice as your catnap zone.

3. Get away from your phone and computer screen, and have a real chat with another human about something other than work.

4. Listen to a mindfulness download or podcast on your phone.

5. Meditate, pray, or reflect.

6. Read from a book that inspires you.

7. Write down everything you are grateful for.

8. Shake it up. I often jump up and down in my office, just to change my energy between clients; it is more effective than a triple dipple Frappuccino.

9. Spray some energizing scents or apply to pulse points. Mint and rosemary are scents that make me feel like I am at a spa.

10. Totally zone out. Stare into space. Drool if you need to. You are entitled.

Ask yourself what you *most need in these ten minutes and how they would best serve you. Any answer is okay as long as it isn't more work.*

Take lunch breaks! Can you imagine cutting out lunch for second-graders so they could keep working on their math assignment? Of course not. But for a lot of folks, lunch has gone the way of recess. Skipping lunch doesn't work, especially if your only breakfast was a quadruple Venti espresso. We don't all have the time or the expense accounts for a two-hour lunch, but we all need to eat. And it would be great if you could combine your lunch with a new environment, get outside, take a walk, breathe some fresh air, move a little, and get some vitamin D—all the things you did on your ten-minute breaks, but longer. Lunches aren't just about giving your body food, but giving your mind a break. "Working while eating lunch doesn't aid recovery," one study by John Trougakos of the University of Toronto reports. Other studies show that working out during our lunch break can also boost productivity (and again, not that productivity is the goal; the goal is self-care, and the nicer you are to you, the more energy, creativity, and chi you have).[27]

It would be nice to find lunch locations that align with your self-care needs—maybe one location for when you need quiet, another for when you need more energy, one more for when you want to be alone, and another still for when you need a hit of luxury. "I sometimes need a bit of comfort after a hard morning at work," the CFO of a major company told me. "A local diner for an occasional comfort meal of grilled cheese and tomato soup goes a long way to make the rest of the day more bearable." That may not sound like a luxury, or even like self-care (she didn't choose kale salad and meditation). But for a woman whose usual lunch is a low-carb salad while perusing a report, this bit of comfort food in a different environment is an act of self-love.

ENJOY YOUR WORK ENVIRONMENT

You may not be able to take a long lunch or pop in for a yoga class before your next staff meeting, but you can create a practice of desk-front activities that remind you to take care of yourself. In most environments, self-care can be done even as you work. Here are some ideas for how:

1. Create a healthy work environment; keep a water bottle and snacks in your desk.
2. Sip water as you work—a hydrated brain is a happy brain.
3. Make sure your chair is ergonomically friendly to your back.
4. Stretch regularly. All that sitting, standing, or whatever it is you are doing for those eight hours will take its toll eventually.
5. Keep fresh flowers on your desk.
6. Play music that energizes you or soothes you, depending on your needs.
7. Keep a picture of people you love on your desk.
8. Find a good lamp whose quality of light isn't energy depleting.
9. Investigate whether a standing desk is a good option for you.
10. Get that eye checkup! New glasses might help you see with less strain.

TAKE OPPORTUNITIES TO LEARN

When talking to other therapists who are complaining of burnout, I am as likely to suggest booking a continuing education class or attending a conference as I am to advise taking a weekend away. All the continuing education I do invigorates my work, primes the pump of passion, and goes a long way to burn off burnout. I am always reading something relevant to my work, which is self-care for my work life, but it isn't as "pump up the volume" as a four-day conference where I am meeting other professionals, learning more, and becoming inspired to get back to work to implement my learning. For me, professionally, this is major four-star self-care.

CULTIVATE RELATIONSHIPS

There are a lot of ways to get self-care from others in the workplace. No man is an island, even if you are a sole proprietor with no employees or an introvert of the highest order. It's important to have people you can moan to, collaborate with, and turn to for support, ideas, and community—not to mention people you can refer to or go to for guidance or grievances. You can find these relationships in peers or professional organizations, or you can turn to a business coach.

MAKE MEANING

Finding meaning in work is absolutely necessary for self-care. Meaning is what shifts you from "I have to go to work" to "I choose to go to work for a clear set of reasons." Knowing why you are doing what you are doing moves you from being a victim into a choice maker, and who wouldn't want that? Actually, a lot of people don't—a lot of people don't want to take responsibility for their choices; they like to lie to themselves that they have absolutely no choice but to do whatever it is they are doing. *I am stuck,* they think. *I am trapped and there is nothing I can do.* It is never true. In every situation, there are choices.

Start by looking at the reason you chose this work in the first place. Why does it matter to you? This is especially important when you are working in a job that is stressful, taxing, and maybe not perfectly satisfying. The president of UNICEF and a pediatric oncologist may have the meaning thing all wired, but most of us need to work hard to understand the meaning inherent in our jobs. Here are some possible answers that might give you back some power:

- I choose this job because it allows me more freedom to spend time with the people I love. Presently, I value time and freedom over money. Even as I complain about the lack of money, I value the freedom more.

- I choose this position because it gives me the flexibility I need so I can continue to work on my dream project. In the past, I have complained about this job, but the truth is that it is allowing me to do what I love on the side. I would, of course, like to be able to do what I love all the time, but for now this is okay.

- I choose this job because the health insurance benefits are very important to me.

- I choose to stay in this job because I know it and am in a comfort zone. I can't handle any discomfort right now.
- I choose this job because it allows me to take care of my family, and that is my highest value.

• • •

If you can't find meaning in the job you have, it may be time to find a new job. Apple co-founder Steve Jobs famously said, "For the past thirty-three years, I have looked in the mirror every morning and asked myself: 'If today were the last day of my life, would I want to do what I am about to do today?' And whenever the answer has been 'No' for too many days in a row, I know I need to change something." If every day in your work you are doing things you hate, things that drain and deplete you, it may be time to start thinking about a change. Quitting your job is one way to do that, but since it is unlikely that you have the financial cushion that Steve Jobs had, it may take some time, planning, and strategizing in order to make a change. Fine. At least you are taking action toward a new and better situation.

If your employer keeps telling you to take care of yourself while overworking you, giving you no time off, telling you to work late, and giving you the stink eye when you talk about taking time off, then you are getting a double crazy-making, no-good message, and that is not okay. Being told to do self-care as a way to compensate for being treated badly in the workplace is not okay. Self-care is not a way to tolerate what is intolerable.

Self-Care at Play

Now that we've brought self-care to work, let's look at the other side—the night to the day. Let's explore how to bring self-care to rest, play, recreation, and relaxation. This, too, is an important skill, and one that many of us are not very good at.

Let's start at the beginning: What is play and why do it?

Play isn't just about leisure activities or things you would tick off on a preferred hobby list; rather, play is an attitude, a vibe, a mood. According to the dictionary, it is to engage in activity for enjoyment and recreation rather than a serious or practical purpose.

But play, it turns out, is so much more. Dr. David Whitebread, cognitive psychologist, scholar, and play expert from Cambridge University, explains: "Play in all its rich variety is one of the highest achievements of the human species, alongside language, culture and technology. Indeed, without play, none of these other achievements would be possible."[28]

We tend to understand that play is necessary for kids' cognitive, emotional, and social development, but it has benefits for adults as well. According to Dr. Stuart Brown, the head of the National Institute for Play, a major function of play is that it takes us out of time. In addition, play has the potential to create community: meeting with others to play golf or Frisbee, sing in a choir, scrapbook, or reenact the Civil War puts you in touch with people who care about what you care about. Dr. Brown also believes that not playing comes with a cost: "What you begin to see when there's major play deprivation in an otherwise competent adult is that they're not much fun to be around," he says. "You begin to see that the perseverance and joy in work is lessened and that life is much more laborious."[29] I also see how *not* playing tends to affect creativity; people who don't regularly allow themselves the pleasures of mindless, purposeless goofiness and freedom to do something just because it is fun, is silly, and feels good are less able to create, or even approach questions creatively.

If, like me, you aren't a natural at play, you might need to think about play in a new way. Play can come through taking up a hobby, playing a sport, or enjoying puzzles or game night; through dance, music, reading, or crafts; but it can also come through unexpected activities like singing in the shower, buying a purple lipstick, going to open houses, popping bubble wrap, or engaging in intermittent happy dances. It isn't the activity that makes it play; what makes something play is approaching the activity with a light, easy, silly, and very un-worky attitude. Nevertheless, we often work hard at what is play for us—getting good at tennis or searching for the perfect fishing spot can look suspiciously like work to the untrained eye.

Here's the truth: only you will know for sure if you are working or playing.

LEARNING TO PLAY AGAIN

As a kid on the playground, you likely didn't need someone to tell you what to do; you just saw those monkey bars, swing, and handball court, and knew which one you wanted to head for. If you don't have the adult versions of merry-go-rounds and a slide in your self-care tool kit, it might take some time and trial to discover what play looks like for you.

A book I regularly recommend to clients who are trying to create and can't get themselves to do so is *The Artist's Way* by Julia Cameron. It's about creativity. You might think that creativity and play are very close cousins that shouldn't be allowed to marry, but this is where that metaphor breaks down, because play and creativity are actually cousins who *can* marry. For creativity to happen there has to be play, and Cameron helps us get back in the game. She asks readers to take their artist-self on weekly dates, and these dates look suspiciously like play. I took my artist, begrudgingly, to a fabric store just to look. I then went to the cemetery where the writer Charles Bukowski was buried and ate cherries while I read to him. And by week three I was at the beach digging the deepest hole I could. Yes, all of this helped me with my writing, and it also got me a whole lot more playful.

My other big play mentor has been my dog. Her absolute insistence that I drop the book and play a rousing and indefinite game of Throw the Monkey is almost always welcome. I can on occasion say no to my need for a play break, but hers? No way. I am not exaggerating when I tell you that I simply couldn't do the work I do if I didn't have a dog—not kidding here. Playing ball with her at the end of the day and watching her silliness is super important for my well-being.

DOING NOTHING

Doing nothing is a type of rest and a type of play that is high-level self-care. A. A. Milne was a man who got stuff done—he studied mathematics at Trinity College at Cambridge and authored the *Winnie-the-Pooh* books—and he said, "Don't underestimate the value of Doing Nothing, of just going along, listening to all the things you can't hear, and not bothering."

Every so often, as I write, I like to stop what I am doing and just let my mind go blank—not in a wise meditative way that Jon Kabat-Zinn might do, no, no. This is just old-fashioned zoning out, chilling out, lollygagging—the kind of thing a teacher might get mad at you for ("Janey, get your head out of the clouds!"). Pico Iyer, the travel writer, put it this way:

> Many of the wisest voices in our tradition, from Whitman to Thoreau, have talked about the virtue of loafing. The less you struggle with a problem, the more it's likely to solve itself. The less time you spend frantically running around, the more productive you are likely to be. It is the pauses in a piece of music that gives the piece its beauty and its shape; always keep pushing forward at full speed, and you end up out of breath.[30]

Vacations: Use them to truly unwind

Hawaii, the lake, a weeklong staycation—you have to have time off. I need one stimulating vacation a year—where I am learning about history or the art of early Peruvian cultures—and one where I do nothing but stare at the water. People in Europe think Americans are wackadoodle for not taking the entire month of August off, and I sort of agree.

Having vacations scheduled is a major element of self-care for me. Knowing that I have a time in the future when I am going to be able to unplug and forget about the demands of everyday life is critical to my ability to do good work. As soon as I get back from one vacation, I have to at least have an idea of when and where I will go next; it helps me, as one friend described it, "make a lot of the sloggy parts of life seem worthwhile to have this sort of thing to look forward to."

And it does. I remember during one particularly harrowing time—I was dealing with a move, going through in-vitro fertilization, and enduring all the stress that comes with both—and I used the promise of a three-day staycation to get me through. Knowing that I would be alone with the latest Harry Potter book made all manner of things tolerable. I do the same thing now. I tell myself, "Sometime this year you will be on a beach, and you will have drinks with umbrellas in them, and you will lie on a lounge chair and you will do nothing." The promise of this is enough to get me through some very hard times.

The research findings about why vacations are beneficial aren't phony baloney and aren't created by the tourist industry to try to trick you into going on a cruise; there are serious medical studies and research that say vacations lead to less stress and to an increase in work productivity.[31] Francine Lederer, a clinical psychologist, observes that "most people have better life perspective and are more motivated to achieve their goals after a vacation." She calls the impact on mental health "profound," while Deborah Mulhern, a psychologist, explains exactly what happens if we *don't* get those breaks: "The neural connections that produce feelings of calm and peacefulness become weaker, making it actually more difficult to shift into less-stressed modes."[32] Eek! Get your calendar out. Let's start with last year. How many vacations did you take? How many days off? Then look at the year ahead and start booking time off.

"But I can't afford it!" you say. I hear you, but there are low-cost ways to sneak in some vacay: one night at a hotel near you or several three-day weekends in a year instead of a two-week marathon that maxes out your credit cards. You can also take staycations and daycations, which can be cheap and cheerful ways to rest and relax. Here's how I do it, planned in advance:

1. The night before, I turn off my alarm clock and turn on my email's "out of town" auto-response.

2. In the morning, I put on a white fluffy robe (feels like a hotel!) and make a special breakfast, starting with fresh-squeezed juice in a fancy glass. I like to mix juices so it feels extra fancy. I ask myself, *what would the Four Seasons do?* Sometimes the answer is that they would mix OJ with cranberry, or sometimes Pellegrino with muddled strawberries and lime. Sometimes the answer is that they would get in their car and drive to the juice store.

3. After pampering myself at breakfast, I break from my normal routine. I take a day trip to a forest or beach, or go for a walk in a new neighborhood or a museum—somewhere that feels new and energizing. (I forget chores and tasks—it's not a vacation if I'm waxing my floors or running over to Home Depot.)

If you need to find a babysitter for the day in order to make your staycation possible, try trading with a friend to give each other a no-cost break or asking a relative for help. Sometimes a day off for no reason is an emergency; you don't have to wait for an *actual* emergency to ask for help.

Our daily rest: Sleep

Sleep is all of a sudden sexy. It seems to have hired the same PR person that kale has. Arianna Huffington is one of its new celebrities. She wrote a book on the subject, *The Sleep Revolution: Transforming Your Life, One Night at a Time.* This is a woman who knows something about success. Here's how she puts it:

> The world provides plenty of insistent, flashing, high-volume signals directing us to make more money and climb higher up the ladder. There are almost no worldly signals reminding us to stay connected to the essence of who we are, to take care of ourselves along the way, to reach out to others, to pause to wonder and to connect from that place where everything is possible.[33]

In her book, Huffington recounts being so sleep deprived that she smashed her face on a desk and then woke up to realize the toll that lack of sleep was taking on her. She now gets eight hours a night.

Sleep deprivation is not just a little bad. It's big bad. It's bad for productivity, bad for performance, and "one of the best predictors of on-the-job burnout," says *New York Times* reporter Tony Schwartz.[34] It's also flat-out bad for our health. Poor sleep has been linked to heart disease, cancer, stroke, obesity, and car accidents.

The following habits can get in the way of sleep:

- caffeine too close to bedtime
- more than one alcoholic drink in the evening
- use of electronic devices within an hour of bedtime
- using your bedroom as anything other than a bedroom; if your bed is a dining table or workstation, then your brain might not get the message that this is a room for sleeping
- watching shows or movies, or reading books that make you anxious, afraid, or agitated; the news might do all of the above
- exercising or eating late

Suffice it to say, sleep is necessary, and if you aren't getting eight hours a night, there may be serious consequences over time.

. . .

If you aren't bringing self-care to work and play, then you are missing out on major-major-major opportunities. It is easy to imagine that achieving self-care through work is about the money your job brings you. But that would be to miss out on at least eight hours a day of self-care-taking in that setting. And, for sure, self-care can't be just about vacations—it has to show up in our sleep habits, our desire for empty space, lollygagging, procrastination, and other things we see as silliness or even laziness. All of that can be self-care.

Even God, according to the book of Genesis, rested on the seventh day. And speaking of God, self-care and spirit are up next—and even if God is not your thing, your spirit still needs to be cared for.

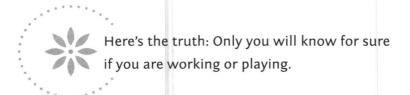

Here's the truth: Only you will know for sure if you are working or playing.

SELF-QUIZ

Self-Care at Work and Play

1. What are you doing for self-care at work? How could you improve that?

2. What do you do at work that is Gray Magic self-care? How do you use work for self-care that you need elsewhere? (Emotional affairs at work? Using work to set boundaries at home? Using work as a distraction from difficult relationships?)

3. Whom do you turn to for support around your work? Peers? Boss? Mentor? Business coach? Do you need more support? What kind?

4. How many sick days have you taken in the last year? What does that indicate to you?

5. What meaning do you make around your work? How would making meaning be an act of self-care for you?

6. Are there parts of your work life that you hate, that drain and deplete you? If so, what small-, medium-, and large-size actions could you take to address this?

7. What is your self-care when it comes to downtime? Rate yourself on a scale of 1 to 10: ___ Sleep ___ Play ___ Vacation ___ Chilling

8. What meaning do you make around sleep, play, vacation, and chilling?

9. How do you create downtime in a way that is Gray Magic self-care?

10. What are you doing now for self-care in all of these categories: Sleep? Play? Vacation? Chilling?

11. How might you improve your care in all of these categories: Sleep? Play? Vacation? Chilling?

12. How much time off have you taken in the last year? What are the numbers?

13. When is your next vacation scheduled? Mark vacation days on your calendar and notice how it affects your mood and your ability to deal with stressors.

Self-Care and Your Spirit

WE ALL NEED SPIRITUAL SELF-CARE. We need it no matter where we fall on the belief continuum, from atheist to agnostic to spiritual to religious. We all need time and space for awe, wonder, gratitude, contemplation, service—something, in other words, that allows us to transcend our ego.

Why? We need a broader view on life, a view beyond our own tiny corner of it. And we need to be reminded of the limits of the human lifespan. We must grapple with the existential truth that someday we'll die, and thereby come to peace with our time here on earth.

In my own spiritual self-care, I am seeking transcendence, mystery, and connection with something beyond words. Some might call that God; others might call it nothing. It doesn't matter much what you call it—I don't happen to call it anything. What lies behind the beauty of ocean waves? Behind the power of music to make us cry, of paintings to make us catch our breath? Behind the awesomeness of dogs? I have no word for that. I do know that when I don't make time for all of the above, life seems flatter and harder, and I am more likely to feel like a hamster on a wheel. Add beauty—whether I'm gazing at a painting or a hummingbird sipping from a flower in my backyard—and my day feels charged.

What about you? What fills you with awe?

• • •

If we grew up with a strong religious tradition, that tradition might still exert a pull on us, even if we're not sure whether we agree with it or not. We might know what our parents or religious leaders said our spiritual self-care *should* look like. And it can be hard to stop approaching our spiritual life in the same way we were taught to do as children. So we march off to temple each week, even though we feel most connected spiritually when we play Mahler at home on the piano. Or we say the prayer we learned when we were eight, even though we feel more aware of God when we're running on a mountain trail.

It's not my place to say whether we're practicing White or Gray Magic in these situations. Spiritual growth can't be codified this way. But it does make sense to notice when our souls *aren't* being fed by a spiritual practice—at least, not at the moment. And let's notice when our souls *do* feel nourished, too. In this chapter, we'll look at some spiritual practices you might find nourishing.

As for Black Magic in this realm, we might agree that self-serving cults would qualify, and any destructive practice that is justified—however falsely— by religion. But again, the framework doesn't really serve us here. A word on addiction, though, which is certainly in the Black Magic territory.

Carl Jung viewed addiction, specifically alcoholism, as a spiritual malady with a thirst for "spirit" at its core. He said as much in a 1961 letter he wrote to Bill W., the co-founder of Alcoholics Anonymous: "Craving for alcohol was the equivalent on a low level of spiritual thirst of our being for wholeness. . . . You see, Alcohol in Latin is 'spiritus' and you use the same word for the highest religious experience as well as for the most depraving poison. The helpful formula therefore is; spiritus contra spiritum." In other words, alcohol counters spiritualism.[35]

When Bill W. wrote back to Jung, he had a story about spiritualism countering alcohol. Bill's friend Rowland had finally found sobriety through spiritual work. Bill listed the practices that made a difference: "The principles of self-survey, confession, restitution, and the giving of oneself in service to others. They strongly stressed meditation and prayer. In these surroundings, Rowland H. did find a conversion experience that released him for the time being from his compulsion to drink."[36]

It's worth noting that spiritual experience—however we define it—can have far-reaching effects in anyone's life.

Doing and Being (Often in That Order)

"You have to *do* things for faith to happen." I heard those words during a sermon at the Washington National Cathedral some years ago. I was a curious visitor, there as much for the architecture and music as the religious content. So the power of the priest's words took me by surprise.

People often claim that they don't have faith, said the priest, as if faith is something one *has* like blue eyes or dimples (okay, those are my examples, not his). But really, he explained, faith is brought about by a set of conditions. You have to create those conditions; you have to *do* things. Faith results from action. He mentioned three actions in particular: being a part of a spiritual community (as an Episcopalian priest, he framed it in those terms), reading time-honored texts that have inspired faith for generations, and being of service to others.

What struck me was the very idea that *action* is necessary to engender faith—not so much the specific actions he was espousing. Spiritual growth often begins with doing things. As Jung said to Bill W., we "walk on a path, which leads to higher understanding."

I believe this truth applies to spiritual self-care as well. We can choose the actions that speak to us. There are many gentle, down-to-earth spiritual practices that can help us on our path to higher understanding. Let's look at eleven of these practices and see how a few everyday people are walking those paths. We'll explore the topics of gratitude, nature, inspiration, art, meditation, ritual, ancestors, awareness of mortality, body, community, and service.

Gratitude

"If the only prayer you said was thank you, that would be enough," said the German philosopher Meister Eckhart. He was born in the thirteenth century, but the wisdom is timeless.

Today, he might keep a gratitude journal. They're a thing now; I hear them recommended in a lot of circumstances, and for good reason. Having gratitude can be a major act of spiritual self-care. It helps us see our life in better focus. Sure, it's easy and even somewhat satisfying to moan and lament the events of the day, but unchecked whining leaves one feeling sad, depleted, and *waaaah*.

Now hear me: I absolutely believe we need room for all our feelings. We need to be able to say, "That sucked, that hurts, I didn't like that"—all of that is important. Repression is not the goal. And I'm not suggesting spinning shit into sunshine; our gratitude list should not be a spiritual con job. It would be a lie to say, "I'm grateful that my co-worker took credit for my idea" or "I'm happy that my child threw up on my brand-new blouse." But let's not see only the bad and ignore all the good. Gratitude isn't just a matter of counting our blessings; it's a way of shifting our attitude from *Shit happens* to *Awesome happens, too!* It gets us out of ourselves and makes us aware of others.

How do you keep a gratitude journal? It's up to you. Some people simply list five to ten things a day, often as a morning or evening ritual. I like to expand on each item a bit. For example:

- I am grateful for my best friend; for feeling heard, cared about, and loved; for feeling inspired and filled with new ideas whenever we talk.

- I am grateful for not hitting traffic today when I drove to my office; for the feeling of ease and peace of not rushing; for actually enjoying the drive.

- I am grateful for the chance to share my work with others and engage with readers.

When I am feeling down or *blech*, sometimes I increase my gratitude practice and do a giant-extravaganza-mega-blast of a hundred items: I'm grateful for antibiotics, for electricity, for the Internet; for Sara Blakely (founder of Spanx); for public libraries; for my ability to see, hear, smell, and taste; for the sound of the crazy woodpecker who is diligently taking down the tree outside my window. You get the idea.

Not surprisingly, research has been done on this subject, and the studies show that consistent gratitude practice makes people feel more optimistic and even visit the doctor less frequently.[37] Some people claim that gratitude changes your vibration, or makes you more likely to let more good into your life. I don't know about that, but I do know that it makes me feel good, and that sharing it with others makes me feel even better. I like to express gratitude to others, including strangers and not-so-strangers. I write thank-you letters and texts telling people how much they mean to me. All of that can be self-care.

Thank you, Meister Eckhart.

"My gratitude practice helps me refocus on all that I have to be grateful for (as it is far too easy to focus on all the other stuff). There is never a time when I sit and enter things in my journal that I don't feel better about my life as it is."—Betsy

Nature

Nature is such a wonderful teacher of self-care. Really, it's a continuing education provider on the topic. And we can find it just about anywhere we are. Sure, it's great to gaze at the ocean, watch a sunset from a hilltop, look at a flower in a garden. But what if we live in a city with no park close by? We can always look up at the sky and clouds. We can look down at the whorls on our own fingertips. We can walk down the street to the nearest tree or patch of grass and focus on that—really look at it. Every bit of nature has its wonder.

For me, trees serve as a metaphor of endurance, constancy, and bending but not breaking. When I see a tree, I sometimes wonder how long it has been there and by how long it will outlive me. There is an intelligence to our world—be that evolution or God or angels. Try gazing at the night sky and really letting yourself be there. When we're paying attention to nature, it can be a high form of meditation and existential awareness. That sense of peace, wonder, and beauty makes us feel more relaxed and alive.

Science backs me up on this. A 2013 *New York Times* article reported that people who live near trees and parks have lower levels of the stress hormone cortisol than those who don't, and that "children with attention deficits tend to concentrate and perform better on cognitive tests after walking through parks or arboretums."[38] In other studies, brain wave readouts show that subjects are more calm and meditative when they view photographs of natural scenes rather than urban scenes.

Exposure to nature can also lower blood pressure, reduce respiratory and cardiovascular illnesses, and restore attention capacity, according to British psychologist Dr. Miles Richardson in a BBC Earth report. The report continued, "But more than that, feeling a part of nature has been shown to significantly correlate with life satisfaction, vitality, meaningfulness, happiness, mindfulness, and lower cognitive anxiety."[39]

As a therapist, I've noticed the same thing. When clients feel disconnected and depressed and hopeless, I often ask them when they last went outside to get some vitamin D in the form of sunshine. I am often met with a blank stare. Anne Frank has an eloquent answer to their doubt: "The best remedy for those who are afraid, lonely or unhappy is to go outside, somewhere where they can be quiet, alone with the heavens, nature and God. . . . Nature brings solace in all troubles."[40]

Seasons can give us powerful metaphors, too. I grew up in LA, so when I moved to Chicago for a while, it was good to learn that after every winter, spring will come, and after the incredible, riotous burst of summer, the leaves will fall. That knowledge changed how I feel when I am in personal winters; I know, even as my inner trees feel bare, that spring will come again.

"When I'm hiking in the woods, when I'm birding, the awe and wonder and quietude of nature sweeps me away from the daily drudgery." —Solange

Inspiration

The word *inspiration* is derived from the ancient Greek word meaning "to breathe." So when we are inspired, we are breathing in Spirit. Inspiration has the power to change our perception, to motivate creativity, and to increase energy and optimism.

Where do we find it? We probably have lots of resources at hand. When I start my day by listening to an uplifting TED Talk, I feel different than I do on days when I start with the news. On the days I start with inspiration from Elizabeth Gilbert, I feel like I've been given an intellectual and emotional vitamin B-12 shot. The news can wait. There is a time and place for learning about the realities of the world, but for me it's not first thing in the morning.

There are myriad ways to be inspired. Here are just a few:

- listening to TED Talks, inspirational sermons or programs, audiobooks, music

- attending support groups, mutual-help meetings, or lectures
- reading biographies, religious texts, poetry—whatever lifts you up
- going to places in nature (as we've discussed)
- seeing human accomplishments, such as feats of engineering or architecture—whatever amazes you

These acts wake up our soul and make us feel peaceful and uplifted.

> *"I read my Bible almost every day, especially Proverbs—like if it's the tenth of the month, I'll read some verses in chapter 10. One of my daily devotional books is Rick Renner's* Sparkling Gems. *And I usually watch Joyce Meyer on TV every morning while getting ready for work."* —Emma

Art

Music, dance, theater, other performing arts, visual art, and even architecture have for centuries been used explicitly to inspire a greater connection to each other, our world, and the divine in all its forms. Art is used in prayer, meditation, ritual, and worship to amplify the experience and to offer a portal into something transcendent. Studies show that a thirty-five-minute visit to an art museum can reduce cortisol levels.[41] But that's never why I go to the museum to see a Rothko painting. For me, Kandinsky had it right when he described what works of art can do for the soul: "They 'key it up,' so to speak, to a certain height, as a tuning-key the strings of a musical instrument."[42]

Spiritual healing can come through witnessing art or from making it yourself. While it is lovely to see the Joffrey Ballet or hear Jennifer Hudson sing a goose-bump-inducing song, doing art on your own is major self-care. Creating a collage, throwing a clay pot, coloring a mandala, dancing in your living room, drumming, strumming your guitar, writing poetry—all can be spiritual self-care. Anything that expands your sense of self beyond the ordinary causes time to fly when you are creating it. It puts you in the now or makes you feel enlarged. Having participated in it, made it, or witnessed it is spiritual self-care. As Pablo Picasso put it, "Art washes away from the soul the dust of everyday life."

"Whenever I am losing my way and can't find the beauty in humanity, I go to a museum. It's not that I think art is an embodiment of something divine. As I see it, art tells us who we are—it's the only evidence that we try to make sense of our world and express ourselves in a way that sets us apart from any other species." —Isabel

Meditation

"To understand the immeasurable, the mind must be extraordinarily quiet, still," said Jiddu Krishnamurti.[43] Study after study shows that meditation is good for us—that it reduces anxiety and improves focus, memory, emotion regulation, and mood. It also increases creativity, productivity, and compassion.[44]

There seems to be almost as many ways to meditate as there are people in the world. You can sit quietly and focus on your breath or a candle or a mantra. You can go to a silent group retreat, do walking meditation, or use an app at your desk. You might use words given to you by a guru, or you might simply wake up and sit in bed and repeat the word *love* over and over until it's time for breakfast.

There are many resources for meditation; one of my favorite writers on this subject is Thích Nhất Hạnh. I don't have a regular traditional meditation practice, but I sometimes listen to his Plum Village Meditation. I relax when I hear his voice, the bells, and his reminder for me to focus: "Breathing in, I know I am breathing in. Breathing out, I know I am breathing out." This exercise gets me out of my mind, my thoughts, and my to-do list, and that is a wonderful thing.

Understanding the immeasurable may take a little longer.

"I meditate because it calms me; it sustains me. It makes the stress of life less stressful, and it makes the joys of life a little sweeter." —Olivia

Ritual

Meditation is a simple form of ritual. But in a religious context, ritual often implies a bit more drama—a bit more staging, right? Still, rituals are simply actions with a special significance that give life a structure and discipline. They organize our spiritual lives amid a changing world, with all the chaos and loss it may bring. Rituals can help ground us, comforting us with a sense of constancy, order, and community.

When our world conveys the sense that it's "every man for himself," rituals work as a magnet, pulling us back together with our tribe, even if it's just for a taco on a Tuesday night. Rituals—especially holidays—connect us with nature, the seasons, our past, our ancestors. Rituals take us out of ordinary time and into a special time. They also serve as rites of passage: think weddings, funerals, even birthday parties.

There are formal rituals such as those of the Christian church (baptism, communion, confession) or the Jewish religion (weekly Shabbat dinners, circumcision, bar and bat mitzvahs). Muslims pray throughout the day. Other people go out to watch the night sky, study the changing seasons in the stars, and connect with the energy of the cosmos.

Rituals of the nonspiritual kind can also be spiritual self-care. Going to the lake for Labor Day, picking apples in the fall, pizza-and-movie night, game night—these all count. Whenever I see my best friend, we reunite by having crab cakes and champagne, and that, too, is spiritual self-care.

I once had a daily ritual of sharing tea on the patio with a roommate. We would meet after work to discuss our days. This wasn't just a habit or a routine—this time was special to us, and we treasured it and rarely let anything get in its way. It may not have looked particularly spiritual to the casual observer but it was, from the making of the tea, to placing it on a tray, to how we tended to the environment where we sat.

Daily rituals might include looking at the newspaper with a child at the breakfast table each morning, walking the dog at sunset, or meditating for five minutes in the dark. You might even have a ritualistic saying. I use the Julian of Norwich prayer: *All will be well and all will be well and all manner of things will be well.* This is my personal soothing mantra from a fourteenth-century Christian mystic that I use daily as spiritual self-care.

> *"I build little altars everywhere. I create rituals celebrating love and the wings of angels. I visit ancient churches as a tourist and enjoy the sacred space, but I'm a Pagan, really, so most of all I spend time amid nature, water especially."* —Renee

Ancestors

I've never seen a book titled *Know Your Ancestors, Change Your Life*, but a lot of folks use this idea as spiritual self-care. I have friends who turn to lost loved ones and ask them for guidance and support. Others I know turn to their ancestors for help, almost as if they are asking their ancestors to intercede on their behalf.

For me, ancestors are a source of inspiration when I feel scared or like *I can't do this*. I think of my forebears who boldly left Ireland over two hundred years ago to start a new life in a country they didn't know. In 1809, one of them, Hannah Allison Cole, entered the area we now know as Missouri along with her husband and nine children. When her husband was killed soon after she arrived, did she run back to her family home in Kentucky? Nope. She stayed in Missouri, built a fort, and started a ferry-crossing business. Hers was the first business license issued there, and later she was the first female property owner in the state. According to one newspaper report, "She once stopped an armed standoff between Native Americans and pioneers by going up to one of the white settlers and placing her own hand over the muzzle of his gun. Both sides gave up, and not one shot was fired."[45] That, ladies and gentlemen, is my forebear.

Knowing I am related to Hannah emboldens me to take risks and do things I think I can't do (if she survived all she did, then I ought to not be moaning about my inconveniences and imagined obstacles). Not all of us have Hannah Cole as a role model, but our forebears can still inspire us. (Tune in to *Finding Your Roots* on PBS with Henry Louis Gates Jr. if you need some genealogical inspiration.) Just the simple fact that you are alive is amazing, proving that you had strong ancestors who survived and endured. Asking family members what they know about your past, or doing your own genealogical research, can introduce to you to people whose DNA you share. Whatever your background, understanding your legacy may add perspective to your own life.

Some of us may run into roadblocks or very scant information. We might be adopted (although we can still feel the heritage of our non-blood families). Or, tragically, there might be historical reasons why we can't trace our lineage, such as slavery or indigenous genocide: facts of our past that are still alive in the present. Still, we can all connect in the abstract with how many generations had to exist, how many events had to happen, for us to exist. That awareness can make us more grateful for the talents and abilities we inherited from our ancestors.

> *"I channel the spirits of my strong female ancestors. Women who raised children and grandchildren during Nazi-occupied France, college presidents, my mother and aunts picked up by Gestapo and leaving their homelands to come to America. I'm always amazed at the strength I get when I focus on these women's spirits and knowing their spirit is in me, too."* —Zoe

Awareness of mortality

Just as our ancestors are gone, soon we will be gone, too. Impermanence is a fact of life, no matter what your belief system. We only get one go-round in this body, which means that no level of self-care is going to keep us from death.

Knowing that you aren't going to live forever is part of self-care. (Some people advise us to live each day as if it were our last, but if we all did that, none of us would eat well, floss our teeth, or vacuum under the bed.) So what's the point of facing the harsh truth that life is fleeting and precious? The point is gratitude. The point is seizing the day.

Whenever I think about death, I want to throw my arms around my favorite people and tell them, "I really love you." Have you ever seen the drunk person at a party who's in that *I really love you, man* phase of inebriation? Well, that's what existential awareness does to me. I feel sad, but very appreciative. It isn't an easy path to those grateful and loving feelings, but I would say it is a path worth treading. It makes us more aware of this extraordinary gift of life we have been given. In feeling that gratitude, we are likely to take better care of what Mary Oliver calls our "one wild and precious life."[46]

Latin cultures dedicate a whole holiday to remembering the fleeting nature of life. *Dia de los Muertos*—the Day of the Dead—is a time for people to think about the loved ones they have lost and their own deaths to come. In Europe in centuries past, the *memento mori* was a painting—or a detail within a larger painting—to remind the viewer that "you are enjoying all this now, but one day you will die." Some fashion designers have used skull images in their clothing. Maybe every age and every culture has its own way of acknowl-edging this existential fact. My friend Janice owns a number of books reflect-ing on death: Sherwin Nuland's *How We Die,* Claire Bidwell Smith's *After This,* Paul Kalanithi's *When Breath Becomes Air.* "Death may be my favorite subject to read about right now," she says. "I find that directly grappling with it is very comforting."

No matter how you go about it, find a way rediscover awe over the very fact of your existence.

> *"When I really need a spiritual fix, I visit the AIDS Memorial Grove in Golden Gate Park. It's sacred ground. I feel the love and energy coming up through my feet; I breathe in the clean, rejuvenating, tree-scented air; I mar-vel at the strength of the trees; I remember so many loved and lost; I am reminded of the unconquerable human spirit. And I go from there into the rest of my day."* —Piper

Body

We discussed self-care and body in chapter 6, but our bodies can be a way into spiritual self-care as well. Yoga is hot, hot, hot in America right now, and I'm not just talking about hot yoga. All forms of yoga allow us to use our bodily experience as a metaphor: breathing into experiences, flowing with experi-ences, and seeing with time that small little movements paired with patience and breath can lead to big change.

Many other physical practices are also intended to help us connect with our spirit: tai chi, qigong, marital arts, labyrinth walking. Even sex: there is ancient tradition of using sex as a doorway to enlightenment. Any physical activity, from golf to skateboarding, can be approached mindfully and can lead to transcendence. (On the other hand, all of these practices can also be turned into mere mechanical activities.) Try reading Gabrielle Roth's *Sweat Your Prayers: The Five Rhythms of the Soul—Movement as Spiritual Practice,* then bring that philosophy to a run, a walk, or even to a game of tennis.

The people who started SoulCycle knew what they were doing: they found a way to bring spirit, community, inspiration, and ritual all into the ordinary exercise of riding your ass off on a stationary bike. Sessions are held in a dim, candlelit room. A community of folks all come together for forty-five sweat-soaked minutes, leaving ordinary time and space behind, and letting themselves be uplifted in a way that is different from "just a workout."

SoulCycle teachers often have inspiring words, too. "There are only two days in the year when nothing can be done," said one teacher. "One is called yesterday and the other is called tomorrow, so today is the right day to love, believe, do, and mostly *live*." Another told me, "The meaning of life is to find your gift. The purpose of life is to give it away." Whenever I emerge from the spin den into the light, I feel empowered, bursting with endorphins, motivated to take those insights into the other twenty-three hours and fifteen minutes of my day.

And you can bring some of that soul to ordinary exercises: light a candle, or chime a bell, or say a prayer, or put on a playlist of music that connects you to transcendence or oneness. Do something to remind yourself that you aren't just moving your body; you're shaping your spirit, too. It applies equally to triathlon training or a tango class. It isn't about the activity; it is about bringing breath and self-awareness to the endeavor.

> *"I take an early morning walk, where I deliberately pace myself and try to take time for the small details in the world around me, as opposed to rush, rush, rush. Very centering and calming."* —Mitzi

Community

We expect to find community in places where people gather for the express purpose of working on their spirit, such as church, temple, or mosque; Twelve Step groups; even a yoga studio. But we might find community in a Zumba class, walking club or book club, or a parent-teacher group. We might find it when we shop regularly at farmers markets or local small businesses, when we join a neighborhood organization, or when we get involved in politics. We might find it by greeting our neighbors when we're out weeding our yard or walking our dog.

Being a part of something bigger than ourselves is spiritual self-care if it gives us a nourishing sense of belonging. The opposite of community is isolation, and isolation leads to despair and loneliness, which can then lead to apathy, indifference, and other social ills: *It doesn't matter if I vote. It doesn't matter if I participate.*

When I lived in Illinois, I found a self-care community when I attended the Episcopal church in Lake Forest, although I wasn't even a member. The truth is that nobody knew my name (to recall that line from the *Cheers* theme song), and I don't know if anyone was particularly glad that I came. But I was always touched by the communion portion of the service. When people gathered around the circular altar, it was as if we are all sitting at the table together, seeing each other's faces. Everyone seemed to be seeking something. I could see suffering as well as joy. Seeing those other nameless faces made me feel that there are other people, lots of other people, who are facing similar life circumstances. In coming together, I believe we all felt less alone.

> *"I run with a great group of ladies at 0-dark-thirty. Our fellowship, and seeing the sun rise, is my spiritual self-care."* —Mariana

Service

Acts of service to benefit others can feed our individual spirit and can, therefore, be acts of self-care. Service can come in all kinds of forms, including volunteering, parenting, or caring for elder parents or loved ones. Those who are interested in social or environmental causes can check out local, regional, and national nonprofits with active volunteer programs. Mark Snyder, a psychologist, says, "People who volunteer tend to have higher self-esteem, psychological well-being, and happiness."[47] Studies also show that volunteering and service lead to improved health and longevity.[48]

We don't have to do a prescribed kind of volunteering in order to receive these benefits. Simply finding ways of being of service, even within our family and friend group, can give us those same soul-satisfying benefits. I like the way Barack Obama put it. "The best way to not feel hopeless is to get up and do something," he said. "Don't wait for good things to happen to you. If you go out and make some good things happen, you will fill the world with hope, you will fill yourself with hope."

> *"It's both service and self-care when I volunteer at the animal sanctuary—I feel so at peace there, like no other place in the world. And I spend time with my aunt, who needs lots of household help. I don't just feed her cat and speed out. We actually spend time talking. If she's in bed, sometimes I*

lay my head against her hip. We lie there and talk, and she strokes my hair. That renews my spirit that was broken when my mom died." —Bella

. . .

As you can see from the variety of voices in this chapter, spiritual self-care takes many different forms. I hope that reading this chapter has given you some spiritual self-care inspiration. Whether or not you consider yourself "spiritual," we all need this kind of self-care to enrich and fulfill our lives.

 We all need time and space for awe, wonder, gratitude, contemplation, service.

SELF-QUIZ

Self-Care and Spirit

1. What are you doing for spiritual self-care?

2. How are you doing in the realm of gratitude? Inspiration, perhaps through nature or art?

3. Do you feel connected with ancestors? With your own mortality? How does your body serve as a portal to your spirit?

4. What spiritual activities feel like self-care to you? What spiritual activities are you doing that *don't* feel like self-care to you?

5. What did you learn from your childhood about spiritual self-care? Is any of it something you want to continue to practice?

6. What habits and rituals do you have that promote your spiritual self-care?

7. What is getting in the way of your spiritual self-care?

8. What habits and rituals would you like to develop that would promote your spiritual self-care?

Afterword

MY HOPE IS THAT YOU NOW KNOW in your bones that self-care isn't a treat, or a reward, or a way to endure what is unendurable. Rather, it's a full-time responsibility, an ongoing investment in yourself. Caring for you is not something you do only when you're exhausted, sick, or burned out—it's a practice that requires continuous awareness. You need self-care when you are tired, hungry, angry, or feeling vulnerable or sad. And you need self-care when you are energetic and happy, too. Self-care goes with you everywhere you go—to work, on vacations, on visits to your in-laws, on big celebration days. Every day, in other words, is another chance to practice self-care. Your whole life, dear one, is an act of self-care. What makes the difference is the quality of that care. Let's look at a few people whose stories capture some of our self-care principles in action.

Nora found the courage to set a boundary. She'd always been kind, easygoing, and agreeable, even in the midst of conflict. In working on improving her self-care, she recognized how that pattern was undermining her. She realized that the most caring thing she could do for herself now was to set a boundary: to speak the truth, communicate her anger to her business associates, and let them know what she required in the future. Here is the miracle: "Those associates realized they were wrong and they apologized, and amends were made," Nora told me. "Prior to looking at self-care this way, I would have thought that the only self-care options were to go to a kickboxing class to deal with the anger and give in to cravings for crunchy tacos so as to process the outrage. It turns out that letting myself stand up for myself was better than tacos. Okay," she admitted, "I had the tacos, too. But this time the tacos were a reward for really taking care of my needs."

Using Maslow's hierarchy of needs, Tony found a new balance in his life. He'd always prioritized his spiritual self-care—meditating, affirming himself, going to Indian sweat lodges—but he neglected his physical health and financial life, and these are the basic building blocks that support our higher pursuits. Tony's problems in those areas were catching up with him. As soon as he began to deal with those basic elements of self-care, he was able to put even more time and energy into his spiritual pursuits.

Hannah used her boundary-setting skills to improve her self-care. She'd always felt that no one ever took care of her, and when she finally found a maid to clean her home, she felt so lucky that she ignored that the maid was doing a bad job. She endured criticisms from her maid—"This house is too small. The closets are bad"—and the relationship grew too personal and not professional enough. Hannah realized that while her solution was good, the execution was not, and she let the maid go. She found another, and soon felt the joy of being well cared for. "You attract what you think you deserve," Hannah said. "People treat you as well as you treat yourself."

Vivian caught her Black Magic self-care habits and turned them around. Her career was stalling, and as her workplace resentment grew, she was turning to addictive behaviors: shopping, emotional affairs, and just one too many glasses of red wine. When she asked herself what she really needed, her answer was an office where she would really love to be. She redecorated her office and transformed it into a place she enjoyed. Soon she began to feel reinvigorated in her work, and her addictive behaviors tapered off. "I was surprised how such a small change impacted how I felt to go to work. I no longer dreaded it," she explained.

For Kate, learning to say no was liberating. A self-admitted people pleaser who served on every committee and volunteered for every opportunity, Kate finally developed a chronic illness. When she sought therapy, she told me she was distraught that she could no longer be all things to all people. Her friends, husband, children, and physicians had all advised her to take better care of herself. But she didn't even know what that meant. In time, it became clear that she had learned self-neglect as a child through the way she was treated by her family of origin. As an adult, Kate went overboard in caring for others, with a secret hope for reciprocity—for people to care for *her*. But when people did offer to help her, she always declined, as she was terrified of being a bother to them. She was exhausted and drained.

Through self-care, Kate discovered some things she really wanted to do that she'd never made time for: a woodworking class, hot yoga, Shabbat dinners. She began to do these things and soon began to accept help from friends and family. "I never thought illness could bring me anything good," she said, "but it has allowed me to stop taking care of everyone else and explore why I am doing this. And now I'm saying no more often. I'm doing more things for me, and there is no guilt."

She did qualify that statement: "I notice that when I hear anyone in need, I still have the impulse to be the hero, to babysit, to make the casserole, to make the hospital visit. But I remember the cost to me and my health to put my superhero, save-everyone-else cape on. Now I really check in and see why I'm tempted to take this action and if this action will feed or drain me. Sometime it does feed me to make the casserole, and sometimes I need to let other people step in. My metric is, does it drain or draw energy? Does it fuel me or fatigue me? I ask myself that before I put my cape back on and try to save the day."

• • •

Your challenge now is to take the approaches we've covered in this book and apply them in your everyday life—just like these people did. Maybe you've already begun to change your relationship with yourself.

So let's review a few basics. Remember our rules of thumb for self-care? Whenever you find yourself wondering, *What's the right self-care thing to do in this situation?* just think of our seven principles:

Principle 1: Self-care is a daily, lifelong practice.

Principle 2: Self-care is self-love.

Principle 3: Self-care means taking personal responsibility.

Principle 4: Self-care means noticing what matters to us.

Principle 5: Self-care requires attention and responsiveness.

Principle 6: Self-care must be realistic to be effective.

Principle 7: Self-care precedes self-fulfillment.

Let these principles guide your choices. Remember, too, that there's no single right answer. It depends on you and on today. What's right, right now?

And if it's helpful, recall our three types of self-care magic. You might ask yourself, *Is straight-ahead White Magic the best investment in myself right now? Would a touch of Gray, an exception to the rule, be refreshing? Or might that Gray choice put me on a slippery slope to destructive Black Magic?* Only you can answer those questions.

Remember your boundary-setting skills, too. Revisit chapter 8 for a step-by-step approach that can bring fresh air and honesty to your relationships. Use those boundary-setting muscles to keep them supple. With better boundaries, you may find yourself with more energy and bandwidth for whatever will bring you joy.

I hope that you are now daring to take better care of yourself. I hope you've accepted that invitation to a life filled with more love and belonging, more self-esteem, more self-actualization. I hope that you see the benefits of higher-quality self-care in every area of your life. I wish you the daily miracle of self-care, the joy that comes from it, and all that it makes possible in your life.

Notes

1. Lev Baesh, "Teaching Jewish Values to Your Children," *Interfaith Family* website, February 2006, www.interfaithfamily.com/relationships/parenting/Teaching_Jewish_Values_to_Your_Children.shtml.

2. Joyce Meyer, "Find the Love, Peace and Joy You're Longing For," *Joyce Meyer Ministries* website, www.joycemeyer.org/articles/ea.aspx?article=find_the_love_peace_and_joy_youre_longing_for.

3. Abraham Maslow, *Motivation and Personality, 3rd ed.* (New York: Harper & Row, 1987).

4. Ibid.

5. Geneen Roth, *Women, Food and God: An Unexpected Path to Almost Everything* (New York: Scribner, 2011), 162.

6. Hans Selye's definition of stress is quoted on the American Stress Institute website, www.stress.org/what-is-stress.

7. Daniel Gilbert, *Stumbling on Happiness* (New York: Knopf, 2006).

8. Sonja Lyubormirsky, "How to Cultivate Happiness?," *Greater Good* website, http://greatergood.berkeley.edu/topic/happiness/definition.

9. Everett L. Worthington, Jr. "The New Science of Forgiveness," *Greater Good* website, http://greatergood.berkeley.edu/article/item/the_new_science_of_forgiveness, and Michael E. McCullough, "The Forgiveness Instinct," *Greater Good* website, http://greatergood.berkeley.edu/article/item/forgiveness_instinct.

10. See Jon Kabat-Zinn, *Full Catastrophe Living: Using the Wisdom of Your Body and Mind to Face Stress, Pain, and Illness, rev. ed.* (New York: Bantam, 2013), Deepak Chopra's work described at the Chopra Center website, https://chopracentermeditation.com, and Thích Nhất Hạnh's work on mindfulness, found at Plum Village Mindfulness Center website, http://plumvillage.org/mindfulness-practice.

11. According to Daphne M. Davis, PhD, and Jeffrey A. Hayes, PhD, the benefits of mindfulness include a decrease in depression, anxiety, physical distress, improvement in overall well-being, emotional regulation, focus, cognitive flexibility, information processing, memory, relationship satisfaction, self-insight, morality, intuition, and fear modulation. Davis and Hayes, "What Are the Benefits of Mindfulness?" *Monitor on Psychology* 43:7, July-August 2012, 64.

12. David D. Burns, *Feeling Good: The New Mood Therapy* (New York: Morrow, 1980), quoted in Mark Morris, *Mental Health for Primary Care: A Practical Guide for Non-Specialists* (Oxford: Radcliffe Publishing, 2009), 20–21.

13. Carl G. Jung, *Memories, Dreams, Reflections* (New York: Vintage Books, 1989).

14. Susan Cain, *Quiet: The Power of Introverts in a World That Can't Stop Talking* (New York: Broadway Books, 2013).

15. Quoted by Susan Biali in "If You Set a Boundary, Expect to Deal with Anger," *Psychology Today*, April 30, 2013, www.psychologytoday.com/blog/prescriptions-life/201304/if-you-set-boundary-expect-deal-anger.

16. Henry Cloud and John Townsend, *Boundaries: When to Say Yes, How to Say No to Take Control of Your Life* (New York: Zondervan, 1992).

17. Crystal Andrus Morissette, *The Emotional Edge: Discover Your Inner Age, Ignite Your Hidden Strengths, and Reroute Misdirected Fear to Live Your Fullest* (New York: Harmony, 2015).

18. Daniell Koepke, Internal Acceptance Movement blog post, January 11, 2013, http://internal-acceptance-movement.tumblr.com/post/40282096370.

19. Nicole Krauss, *The History of Love* (New York: Norton, 2005).

20. Cheryl Richardson, *Take Time for Your Life: A Personal Coach's Seven-Step Program for Creating the Life You Want* (New York: Broadway Books, 1998).

21. Marie Kondo, *The Life-Changing Magic of Tidying Up: The Japanese Art of Decluttering and Organizing* (New York: Ten Speed Press, 2014).

22. Bari Tessler, "How to Take Yourself on a Money Date," *BariTessler.com*, October 24, 2012, http://baritessler.com/2012/10/how-to-take-yourself-on-a-money-date/.

23. Shawn Achor and Michelle Gielan, "Resilience Is About How You Recharge, Not How You Endure," *Harvard Business Review*, June 24, 2016, https://hbr.org/2016/06/resilience-is-about-how-you-recharge-not-how-you-endure.

24. Ivan Robertson and Cary Cooper, *Well-being: Productivity and Happiness at Work* (New York: Palgrave Macmillan, 2011), p. 75. See also Jane Keep, "Self-Care at Work Makes Sense—Why Is It Not Common Practice?" at Unimed Living website, www.unimedliving.com/work/self-care-at-work/self-care-at-work-makes-sense-why-is-it-not-common-practice.html.

25. Jon Hamilton, "Think You're Multitasking? Think Again," National Public Radio's *Morning Edition*, October 2, 2008, www.npr.org/templates/story/story.php?storyId=95256794.

26. Tony Schwartz, "Relax! You'll Be More Productive," *New York Times*, February 9, 2013, http://www.nytimes.com/2013/02/10/opinion/sunday/relax-youll-be-more-productive.html?.

27. John Trougakos, study cited in Joe Robinson's "The Secret to Increased Productivity: Taking Time Off," *Entrepreneur,* October 2014, www.entrepreneur.com/article/237446.

28. David Whitebread, *The Importance of Play,* report written for Toy Industries of Europe, April 2012, www.importanceofplay.eu/IMG/pdf/dr_david_whitebread_-_the_importance_of_play.pdf.

29. Sami Yenigun, "Play Doesn't End with Childhood: Why Adults Need Recess Too," National Public Radio's *All Things Considered,* August 6, 2014, www.npr.org/sections/ed/2014/08/06/336360521/play-doesnt-end-with-childhood-why-adults-need-recess-too.

30. Pico Iyer, quoted in interview with Jennifer Haupt, "Pico Iyer: The Art of Doing Nothing," *Psychology Today,* Nov. 30, 2014, www.psychologytoday.com/blog/one-true-thing/201411/pico-iyer-the-art-doing-nothing.

31. Studies cited in "Road Trip! Health Net Points Out the Health Benefits of Vacations," *HealthNet* website, www.healthnet.com/portal/home/content/iwc/home/articles/health_benefits_of_vacations.action.

32. Lederer and Mulhern are quoted in Kristi Hedges, "The Best Reason Ever to Take a Two Week Vacation," *Forbes,* June 25, 2013, www.forbes.com/sites/work-in-progress/2013/06/25/the-best-reason-ever-to-take-a-two-week-vacation/#14c1c6dc5820.

33. Huffington, Arianna, *The Sleep Revolution: Transforming Your Life, One Night at a Time* (New York: Harmony, 2016).

34. Tony Schwartz, "Relax! You'll Be More Productive," *New York Times,* February 9, 2103, www.nytimes.com/2013/02/10/opinion/sunday/relax-youll-be-more-productive.html?.

35. Quoted in James B. Nelson, *Thirst: God and the Alcoholic Experience,* 1st edition (Louisville, KY: Westminster John Knox Press, 2004), 28.

36. Quoted in Benjamin Kissin, *Treatment and Rehabilitation of the Chronic Alcoholic,* softcover reprint of 1977 edition (New York: Springer, 2013), 453.

37. Harvey B. Simon, MD, "Giving Thanks Can Make You Happier," *Harvard Men's Health Watch,* November 2011, www.health.harvard.edu/healthbeat/giving-thanks-can-make-you-happier.

38. Gretchen Reynolds, "Easing Brain Fatigue with a Walk in the Park," *New York Times,* March 27, 2013, http://well.blogs.nytimes.com/2013/03/27/easing-brain-fatigue-with-a-walk-in-the-park/.

39. Jeremy Coles, "How Nature Is Good for Our Health and Happiness," *BBC Earth,* April 20, 2016, www.bbc.com/earth/story/20160420-how-nature-is-good-for-our-health-and-happiness.

40. Anne Frank, *The Diary of a Young Girl* (New York: Doubleday, 2010).

41. Abe Bergado, "Science Shows Art Can Do Incredible Things for Your Mind and Body," *ArtsMic.com,* December 15, 2014, https://mic.com/articles/106504/science-shows-that-art-is-having-fantastic-effects-on-our-brains-and-bodies#.JtJmcht9.

42. Wassily Kandinsky, *Concerning the Spiritual in Art,* revised edition (Dover Publications, 1977), 2.

43. Quoted on "Jiddu Krishnamurti" on *Goodreads* website, www.goodreads.com/author/show/850512.Jiddu_Krishnamurti.

44. Emma Seppala, "How Meditation Benefits CEOs," *Harvard Business Review,* December 14, 2015, https://hbr.org/2015/12/how-meditation-benefits-ceos.

45. Kat Teraji, "Putting 'Great' in Grandmother," *Gilroy* (California) *Dispatch,* March 10, 2011, www.gilroydispatch.com/news/teraji-putting-great-in-grandmother/article_0785c9bf-c46f-5c5c-a25c-8e97a86ea295.html.

46. Mary Oliver, "The Summer Day," in *New and Selected Poems* (Boston: Beacon Press, 1992), 94.

47. Phillip Moeller, "Why Helping Others Makes Us Happy," *US News and World Report,* April 4, 2012, http://money.usnews.com/money/personal-finance/articles/2012/04/04/why-helping-others-makes-us-happy.

48. Stephanie Watson, "Volunteering May Be Good for Body and Mind," *Harvard Health Publications,* June 26, 2013, www.health.harvard.edu/blog/volunteering-may-be-good-for-body-and-mind-201306266428.

About the Author

Tracey Cleantis is a licensed marriage and family therapist and the author of the critically acclaimed book *The Next Happy: Let Go of the Life You Planned and Find a New Way Forward*. She lives in Pasadena, California, with her fiancé, Keith, and her dog, Lily.

About Hazelden Publishing

As part of the Hazelden Betty Ford Foundation, Hazelden Publishing offers both cutting-edge educational resources and inspirational books. Our print and digital works help guide individuals in treatment and recovery, and their loved ones. Professionals who work to prevent and treat addiction also turn to Hazelden Publishing for evidence-based curricula, digital content solutions, and videos for use in schools, treatment programs, correctional programs, and electronic health records systems. We also offer training for implementation of our curricula.

Through published and digital works, Hazelden Publishing extends the reach of healing and hope to individuals, families, and communities affected by addiction and related issues.

For more information about Hazelden publications,
please call **800-328-9000**
or visit us online at **hazelden.org/bookstore**.

Also of Interest

The Next Happy
Let Go of the Life You Planned and Find a New Way Forward
Tracey Cleantis

When the best option is to let go of the life you planned for yourself and find a new path, a world of possibilities can surprisingly open up. Learn whether it's time to let go, and if so, how to move through your grief and find your way forward.
Order No. 7768; ebook EB7768

The Gifts of Imperfection
Let Go of Who You Think You're Supposed to Be and Embrace Who You Are
Brené Brown, PhD, LMSW.

This *New York Times* best-seller by a leading expert on shame blends original research with honest storytelling and helps readers move from "What will people think?" to "I am enough."
Order No. 2545; ebook EB2545

A Kinder Voice
Releasing Your Inner Critics with Mindfulness Slogans
Thérèse Jacobs-Stewart

A well-known mindfulness meditation teacher and author offers one of the most effective approaches to calming a self-critical mind.
Order No. 9798; ebook EB9798

For more information about Hazelden publications,
please call **800-328-9000**
or visit us online at **hazelden.org/bookstore**.